DESIGN MAKE QUILT

HEATHER BLACK

MODERN

Taking a Quilt from Inspiration to Reality

stashBOOKS®

an imprint of C&T Publishing

PUBLISHER: Amy Barrett-Daffin

CREATIVE DIRECTOR: Gailen Runge

ACQUISITIONS EDITOR: Roxane Cerda

MANAGING EDITOR: Liz Aneloski

EDITOR: Karla Menaugh

TECHNICAL EDITOR: Debbie Rodgers

COVER/BOOK DESIGNER: April Mostek

PRODUCTION COORDINATOR: Zinnia Heinzmann

PRODUCTION EDITOR: Alice Mace Nakanishi

ILLUSTRATOR: Aliza Shalit, unless otherwise noted

PHOTO ASSISTANT: Lauren Herberg

PHOTOGRAPHY by Estefany Gonzalez
of C&T Publishing, Inc., unless otherwise noted

Library of Congress Cataloging-in-Publication Data

Names: Black, Heather, 1976- author.

Title: Design, make, quilt modern : taking a quilt from inspiration to reality / Heather Black.

Description: Lafayette, CA : Stash Books, [2021]

Identifiers: LCCN 2020029468 | ISBN 9781617459573 (trade paperback) | ISBN 9781617459580 (ebook)

Subjects: LCSH: Patchwork--Patterns. | Quilting--Patterns. | Textile design, Abstract.

Classification: LCC TT835 .B5113 2021 | DDC 746.46/041--dc23

LC record available at https://lccn.loc.gov/2020029468

Printed in the USA

10 9 8 7 6 5 4 3 2 1

DEDICATION

This book is dedicated to my parents, Cory and Joan,
and my "Missy Pie," CoraJoan, for all their support.

Aurifil thread

Photo by Heather Black

ACKNOWLEDGMENTS

Thank you to Paintbrush Studio Fabrics for providing all the fabric for the sample projects, to Aurifil Thread for meeting all my thread needs, and to Hobbs Batting for their generously giving me all the batting required for the book.

I would also like to personally thank God for making me who I am and giving me the opportunity to be creative and make quilts for His glory.

"This is the message which we have heard from Him and declare to you, that God is light and in Him is no darkness at all. If we say that we have fellowship with Him, and walk in darkness, we lie and do not practice the truth. But if we walk in the light as He is in the light, we have fellowship with one another, and the blood of Jesus Christ His Son cleanses us from all sin." —1 John 1:5–7 (NKJV)

CONTENTS

93

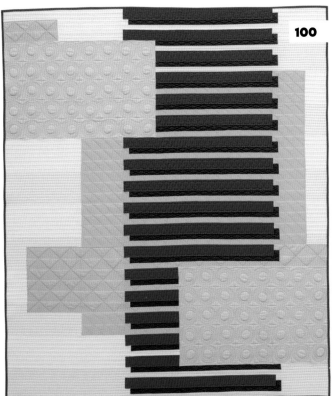

100

107

119

INTRODUCTION

Everyone can design quilts, even you! This book will show you ideas and techniques that will help you design your own quilt by taking small steps—from recognizing design inspiration and your own likes and skills to learning some tips and tricks you can use to enliven and balance your quilt design.

While I focus on modern quilts, the techniques you'll discover in this book will help you design whatever style of quilt you want to make.

It's easy to think you can't design, it's too hard to design, or your designs are not as good as others. But the truth is that by following, or in some cases breaking, simple design rules, your quilt designs will come to you more easily and look sharper. I use easy-to-understand terms and common sense to communicate tried-and-true design strategies.

Just in case you were thinking you don't have enough art background or knowledge to design your own quilts, I want to share a bit about my design and artistic background. I have no formal art education beyond public school and an occasional summer art class, but I do have a curiosity about design. When I was eight or nine, I was invited to go to a painting class with a friend. The teacher was fabulous, and I went back a half dozen times. This is as close to a formal art instruction as I ever received. Not that impressive, is it? But the flame was lit, and I wanted to learn more, do more.

You might be asking yourself, *Why should I design my own quilts?* As quilters, we can be hit with inspiration anywhere. Have you ever said to yourself, *I can make that into a quilt!*, or wanted to make a quilt for a special occasion or person and just couldn't find a pattern to work? These are both great opportunities to design your own quilt.

A stack of my completed quilts!

Photo by Heather Black

Or perhaps you are thinking of entering quilt shows or starting your own line of quilt patterns. Many shows prefer original work over quilts created from another quilter's design. Whatever your reason, designing your own quilt is very fulfilling and a chance to exercise your creativity in a craft that you love.

If designing your own quilt is so amazing, why do we have quilt patterns? Patterns are a great tool for expanding your quilting and designing skills. A particular pattern may have a technique—for example, curve piecing—that you've never tried before, and a step-by-step pattern is the perfect way to learn. You also could choose a pattern because you love the design and want to make "that quilt." Patterns are perfect for quilt-alongs and bonding with other quilters, so don't throw out your patterns. There is a time and place for both original work and patterns.

The quilt design doesn't stop when the quilt top is complete. This book also includes how to take the next step and custom quilt your design. Custom quilting is a great way to build and add another layer of design and gives you the ability to personalize any quilt. By the end of the book, you will be able to go from inspiration to binding with a quilt that is uniquely yours.

Design and make more quilts that are 100% you!

Quilts made by Heather Black

Photo by Heather Black

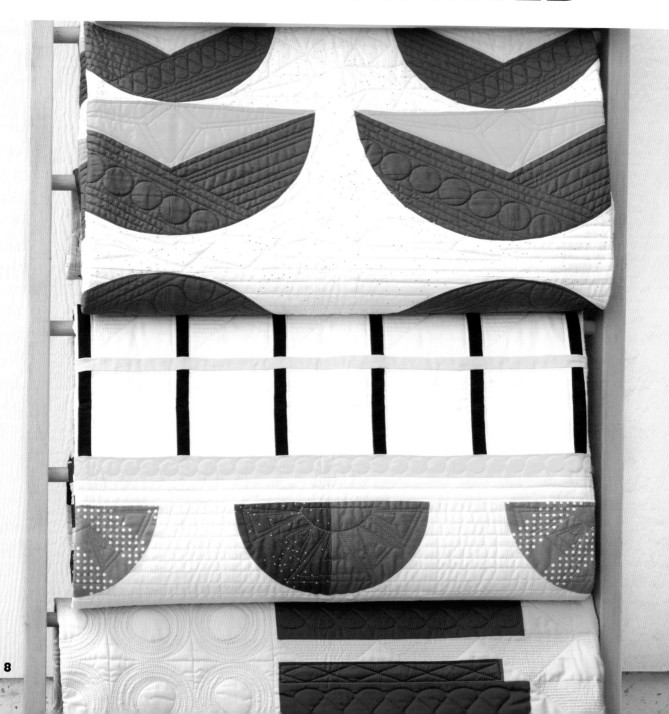

GETTING STARTED

TOOLS OF THE TRADE

You wouldn't paint a house with a box of crayons, and it's just as important to design quilts with the right tools. There is no reason to start off by creating more work than there needs to be, and using the right tools is the first step to success. Here is what I recommend.

Low-tech design tools

Photo by Heather Black

LOW-TECH TOOLS

Some of the must-haves:

- Graph paper
- Pencil
- Eraser
- Clear plastic ruler
- Calculator
- Colored pencils

Most of us have these items around our house or can find them at the local grocery or "all-in-one" store. Even if you have a ruler around the house, buy a clear or translucent ruler. It will make designing easier if you are able to see the lines under the ruler, and it also comes in handy when working on a quilting plan.

I started designing by rummaging around storage boxes to find that one pad of graph paper I knew I had somewhere. I did eventually find it, but ended up buying a new pad of graph paper that was more suitable for quilt design.

Depending on what you are designing, you may need different graph papers. There are graph papers divided in units of 10, great for the metric system, and others in units of 8, perfect for the imperial system of measurement. There are graph papers for hexagons, triangles, and even wedges. Having a collection of graph papers for the quilts you design most often will make it easier to translate any inspiration into a quilt.

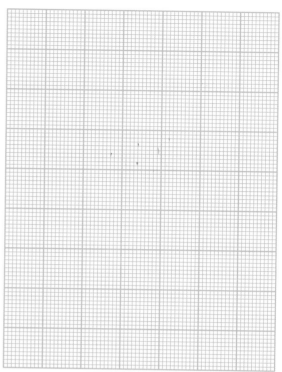

Metric graph paper

HIGH-TECH TOOLS

Even though working with paper and pencil is perfectly acceptable, it can be fun and more convenient to use software for design.

My start to designing with a computer program came about in an unexpected way. After college, the company I worked for needed labels for their pool chemicals. I was the assistant to the marketing director, so they bought me a copy of Photoshop 5.5 and asked me to make them. I had no idea what I was doing; I had used Paintbrush in college to make wallpapers for my laptop, but that was just for fun. (I have to add they also asked me to translate an MSDS—Material Safety Data Sheet—from French to English after they'd heard I took French in high school and had been to France twice, so I'm not sure they were using the best judgment while delegating tasks to me.) That aside, I set out to make labels and relied heavily on whatever design I'd picked up on the way. From that time forward I have used Photoshop to design, even quilts.

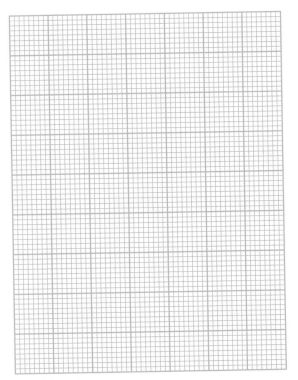

Imperial graph paper

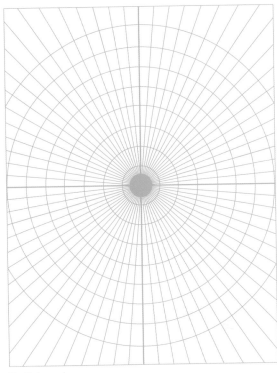

Radial graph paper

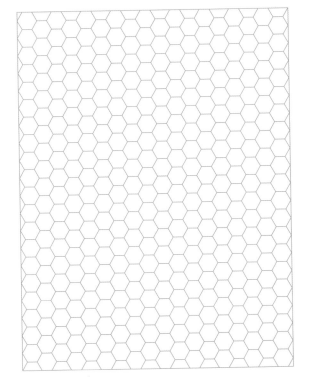

Hexagon graph paper

Triangle graph paper

Adobe Photoshop is what I'm comfortable with, but there are plenty of design programs out there. I also use EQ8, a specialized computer program for quilt designing by Electric Quilt Company, to create templates for my patterns and calculate fabric requirements for designs. Almost any program that has a grid and you can create shapes in will work, so it's important to choose something that you are comfortable using.

Many designers use Adobe Illustrator to design quilts. A benefit to Illustrator is that it is vector-based and not pixel-based. Vectors allow the image—or quilt, in this case—to be resized without losing any resolution or details of that image. Here are some of the programs that can be used to design quilts:

- Adobe Illustrator
- Adobe Photoshop
- Electric Quilt 8 ("EQ8")
- Microsoft Paint
- Pixelmator (Mac only)
- PreQuilt (online)
- Quilt-Pro

This is nowhere near a complete list nor is it an endorsement for one program over another. What is important is to use the program that works well for you. For example, when Illustrator came out it was very similar to Photoshop, so I never used it. But as the two programs became more advanced, they diverged from each other. I tried to switch to Illustrator a couple years back, but just couldn't get used to all the different features, so I went back to Photoshop. There's nothing wrong with Illustrator, but I am comfortable with Photoshop. That's what's important if your goal is to design and make more quilts successfully.

High-tech design tools

Photo by Heather Black

DESIGN WALL

Quilt designing doesn't always require that the quilt be pre-planned and laid out before you cut your first strip of fabric. If you are more of a design-as-you-go or an improv piecer, it's essential that you have a design wall.

Design walls are a good way to keep your quilt from taking on characteristics or an appearance that you weren't intending. Also, it is easier to experiment with design tips and tricks when you can manipulate the units of the quilt on a design wall opposed to while you are sewing.

Design walls don't have to be fancy. Some batting or flannel on a wall is enough to hold your blocks or units. Some piecing, especially paper piecing or piecing with an abundance of seams, will weigh more and the simple batting design wall won't work— gravity overcomes the coefficient of friction and the blocks fall! In this case, building a design wall that you can pin fabric to will work best. There are plenty of tutorials on the internet for making this type of design wall, from con-structing a faux wall to using a foam-core board. There are even felt tiles that will work as a design wall. Plenty of options abound to fit a range of needs and spaces.

Photo by Heather Black

DESIGN IS ALL AROUND YOU

When you go about your day, there are design ideas and tips all around you. You'll be surprised how useful all those everyday design tips can be when you store them away to use later.

BE A HUNTER/GATHERER

The best way to hunt and gather design tips and tricks is to be on the lookout for them. This doesn't have to consume your day with hours of research. Simply keeping your ears and eyes open will work.

After I started oil painting in elementary school, I started watching Bob Ross's *Joy of Painting* as much as I could, which was usually only once or twice every few months. It was easy to be entertained with the fun way he had of talking or the photos of his squirrels, but he also explained why he did the things he did. This created a hunger in me to answer the question, "Why?" Why did the tree go there and not there? Why are water lines always horizontal? Why that color and not the other color? I was on the hunt for design techniques and I didn't even know it. Do I recommend you go back and watch all the Bob Ross you can find? Of course, because it's fabulous, but it's not necessary. The important thing is to ask why. Whether you're watching Bob Ross or a design show on HGTV, or noticing other art in your everyday life, remember to ask why.

If you want more structured learning, there are plenty of resources on fine art and art history. I can still recall works of art that made an impression on me in my art history class in college (a requirement of my liberal arts education). But what I remember most is thinking about why that piece of art made an impression.

It is helpful to have a basic understanding of different periods in art history and what influenced them.

For example, I often am asked what makes a quilt modern. I typically answer with another question: "Do you know what modern art is?" Most people do. They can reference a sculpture, painting, or even a piece of furniture that fits that description. That's when I say that if a quilt will look at home with modern art, it's a modern quilt. This is not an exhaustive definition, but it helps.

Having some knowledge of art history will help in designing your own quilts. If you know you're making a modern quilt, it may not be useful to your design to use a color palette more at home in the Renaissance period.

Another great option for finding design tips—observe your world.

Look around your everyday life but remember to ask yourself why. I really like that house. . . . *Why?* Wow, that ad caught my attention. . . . *Why?* I can't help but smile when I see that chair. . . . *Why?* By taking a few seconds to ask yourself why you react to things in your everyday life, you will be hunting and gathering design tricks and tips without even realizing it.

Eavesdropping doesn't hurt either. Every good hunter is a good listener. When I was twelve or so, my mom took me to a party store. I remember a conversation between a lady buying balloons and the lady filling balloons. The customer was

Early oil painting of tree at Butchart Gardens,
Vancouver, British Columbia, by Heather Black

Photo by Heather Black

struggling to choose balloon colors, and the employees simply said, "Pick any three colors and they will go together." They then proceeded to mix and match balloon colors and to the amazement of the customer, and myself, it worked! Looking back at it, there were some parameters that allowed the lady's balloon theory to work; for example, all the balloons had a similar saturation of color and similar tint/shade. But keeping my ears open for design tips led me to a color theory. Remember that people everywhere and in all walks of life can be excellent sources for design tips.

Another good way to glean design tips and tricks is to pay attention to other quilters. Quilters love looking at another quilter's work. Next time you're at a guild meeting, quilt show, or browsing online and you come across that quilt that stops you in your tracks, don't forget to ask yourself, why? This doesn't mean you have the same style or taste in colors, but ask yourself why that design is so striking or attention-getting. Is it how they placed the shapes or is it how the colors interact with each other? I can't stress it enough—ask why! You will be surprised how much your own designs will change and grow as a quilt designer/maker by asking why you like the quilts you do.

STORING DESIGN TRICKS FOR LATER

One of the least complicated ways to store and keep design tips is to carry a small notebook with you so you can store the tip right away. This is a good way to keep all the design tips in the same place and easy to access.

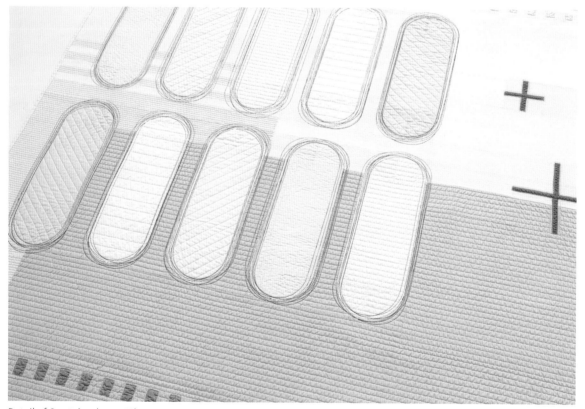

Detail of *Swatches* (page 52)

Another, and probably more popular, way to store up your ideas is to capture them on your smart phone. Technology is amazing. If you are around the same age as me, you'll remember the original 8-inch floppy discs that typically held about 80 kilobytes of data. Today a basic smart phone hold 64 gigabytes, that's 64,000,000 kilobytes or 800,000 floppy discs—staggering. Our phones are amazing, a minicomputer at our beck and call, to store all the design tips and tricks we come across. Take a picture, take a screen shot, scribble down a note, share ideas, or even leave yourself voice memos with a swipe or a click. The one thing that has escaped me with my smart phone is an easy way to keep all my tips and trick gathering organized, which may not be the case for everyone.

When it comes down to it, whether you have a good memory, an organized notebook, or mad smart-phone skills, there is a storage option that will work for you. Figuring out what option works best for you will make you more successful at storing up all the tips and tricks you pick up on the way.

APPLYING TIPS AND TRICKS TO QUILT DESIGN

You've made it through hunting and gathering and you've stored all you've gleaned from your experiences, but how in the world does this help you design a quilt? In the coming chapters, I will go over design techniques in easy-to-understand, common sense terms that you will be able to match up the tips and tricks you gathered. This will help you figure out how to apply what you've learned in this book and along the way.

Detail of *Trellis* (page 64)

DESIGN WHAT YOU KNOW AND LOVE

GET TO KNOW YOURSELF

It seems like a simple concept—designing what you know and love—but how many times have quilters picked up a pattern or bought a quilt kit they were "in love with at first sight," then never finish or even start it? Many times, this is because the quilter didn't know their skills, likes, and/or dislikes. Even though I can love and respect quilts of all techniques and styles, I don't make quilts of all techniques and styles because I know what I can and cannot do, what I like and don't like. I won't even design a quilt that I know I don't have the skill to make or won't like. If I did, I would be setting myself up for failure. Knowing your creative skills, likes, and dislikes can lead to quilting success.

Skill Inventory

Taking an inventory of your skills is a great first step to designing a quilt. You're not going to want to design a shape or unit that is achievable only with improv curve piecing when you don't know how to piece improv curves. Making a check list of quilting skills is a good exercise to consider before designing a quilt.

Close-up of *Sunset Horizons* (page 41)

Photo by Heather Black

Fortunately, skills can be expanded and fine-tuned. Even if you were only able to check off a few of the skill listed, that doesn't mean you won't someday check off all of them. A great way to expand your skill set is to buy a pattern with a skill you are interested in developing, or purchase a book that can help you through the process step by step. This differs from buying a quilt pattern impulsively without first knowing if you will be able to make it, or even like to make it. The desire to learn is an excellent motivator, so you are more likely to use that pattern if you bought it to learn a technique. At this point, you may want to make a separate list of techniques you would like to learn as you grow as a quilter.

TECHNIQUES AND STYLES

Likes and Dislikes

Now it's time to inventory likes and dislikes—or favorites and less-than-favorites, to use gentler terms.

> *Just because you know how to perform a task doesn't mean you enjoy or even like it.*

I know how to fold laundry, but I do not like to fold laundry. This attitude is true of quilting techniques too. I know how to sew inset circles, but it's not my favorite technique. Likes and dislikes include aspects of design that reach beyond skills—for example, colors. I can honestly say I like all colors, but I definitely have favorites. I love pink; pink sneaks into almost all of my designs. Conversely, I'm not as fond of cool color palettes and very seldom design only with them. When I do include cool colors, they are very rarely the center of attention in the design and tend to be more on the warm side of cool. I'll talk more about warm and cool colors later (page 50).

Sewing Skills

- ✗ Straight piecing
- Curve piecing
- ✗ Piecing triangles
- ✗ Piecing hexagons
- ✗ Y-seams
- Paper piecing
- Appliqué
- ✗ English paper piecing
- ✗ Embroidery
- ✗ Improv sewing
- Hand sewing/piecing
- Binding
- ✗ Facing

Inventory *✶

Skills:

✗ Straight piecing

Curve piecing

✗ Triangles

✗ Paper piecing

✗ Improv

My Favs:

♡ HST, HRT, curves, circles, solids, geometrics, subtle prints, warm colors, triangles, stripes …

Not My Favs:

 Improv, paper piecing, red-and-white, blue-and-white, polka dots, micro piecing, alternative substrates …

Some likes and dislikes are so ingrained in our design style that, without knowing it, we include these likes and exclude these dislikes. But some likes and dislikes are harder to identify. If you are struggling with a design, it might be because you're hanging on to a dislike. For that reason, it is important to take a moment and inventory your likes and dislikes.

Skills Worksheet

Use the space below to inventory your skills. This can also be used to list what skills you'd like to learn or explore in the future.

Likes:

_____

_____

_____

_____

_____

Dislikes:

_____

_____

_____

_____

_____

If you are still uncertain about what you may or may not like, a good starting place is to think about the quilts you've made. Which quilts did you enjoy making? Which quilts were never finished? Which quilts made you proud to say, "I made that?" Which quilts went straight to storage without you sharing them?

Just as skills can change and grow, likes and dislikes can change over time. As my mother can tell you, I used to kick and scream over all the pink dresses she made me wear and now I can't get enough of pink. The more you are aware of your likes and dislikes the more you will naturally select design elements you like without fighting over or even giving thought to your current dislikes.

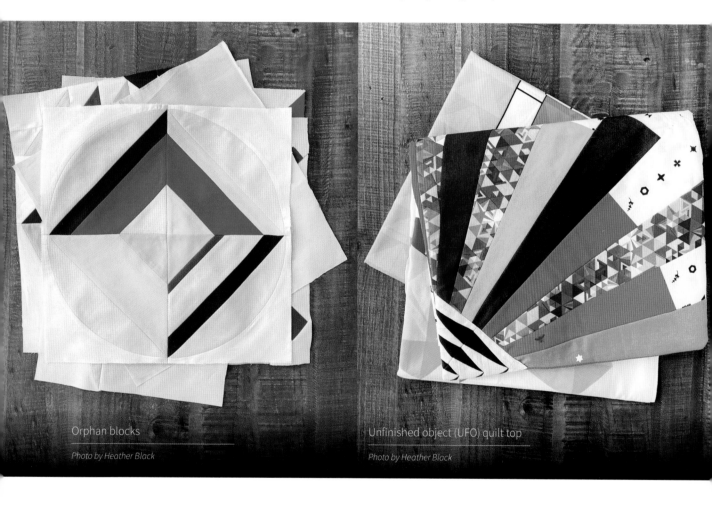

Orphan blocks

Photo by Heather Black

Unfinished object (UFO) quilt top

Photo by Heather Black

GO EASY ON YOURSELF

Designing quilts can be a really exciting adventure, but as in all adventures, not everything will go as planned. You may run out of fabric, you could realize there's no way to execute your design, or you might tire of a color halfway through piecing. It's always good to remember to go easy on yourself. These bumps and bends in the road don't make you a bad designer or quilter. All it makes you is normal. Everyone runs into roadblocks, but you can find joy in the problem solving.

Don't waste time comparing yourself to other designers or quilters; comparisons never end well.

Instead set goals for yourself and take steps to accomplish those goals. They could be design goals, piecing goals, or quilting goals. They could be career goals like entering an international quilt show or writing your first pattern. It's your own personal growth chart. It doesn't matter if a quilt designer you know is ahead of you or behind you; what matters is that you keep growing at your pace. Take time to look back at some of your first quilt designs and see how you've changed. Styles change, likes and dislikes change, and your skill level will change. This is the best marker, not comparing your work to others.

Something else will happen after you complete and share your own original quilt—people will like it. They will say, I really like this bit or that feature and knowing all the reasons why you included those details makes all the work worth it. What's great about designing your own quilt and making all of those design decisions is that the overall of look of your quilt will leave a lasting-favorable impression. Accept compliments about your designs without pointing out your mistakes. "Thank you, I appreciate that" is a perfectly acceptable answer to any compliment.

No one is going to see all the little missteps you know about because your hovered 10″ above your quilt from beginning to end. They will see how put-together your design is and all the work you put into it.

Remember that all quilters were beginners at one point.

If there is that quilter in your life who insists on pointing out all the flaws in your work—I have a few of those—be kind to them and move on. The problem isn't your work; it's with them.

My hope is that you will make quilts that are decidedly you. One of the greatest compliments I receive when showing a new design is that the person knew it was my quilt before knowing for certain who made it. I want designers to find their creative style and voice. Applying simple design techniques while coming up with your next quilt will allow your voice to show through in the design.

Believe in your designs and enjoy the process without worrying about perfection. Go easy on yourself!

DESIGN BASICS *for* MODERN QUILTS

INSPIRATION

Inspiration can come from anywhere. It can be something you see, something you feel, or something you experience. Most of my inspiration comes from my memories. *Road Trip* (page 55) is inspired by all the family road trips we took when I was growing up and still take together. Almost every summer, as a kid, my family would take a road trip, usually with our tent trailer in tow. We traveled all over the Pacific Northwest. It's taking a little moment, remembering my road trips, and saving it up that creates the inspiration for later projects.

One of the most common ways to be inspired is to look at the world as a possible quilt. Much like the Tootsie Roll commercial song … "Whatever it is I think I see, becomes a Tootsie Roll to me," your world can become a quilt. A common phrase that I say to myself is, *I can make that a quilt.* When you start to see the environment around you in terms of how it translates into a quilt, you will have an abundance of inspiration.

You don't have to spend your entire time with "quilt-colored" glasses on. But every once in a while, take time to look for quilts—they pop up in the most unique place. This is a good time to use a design tips notebook to jot down a quick inspiration or idea or a quilt. I've frustrated myself in the past by letting an inspiration pass by and not being able to remember it later. Having something handy to collect the inspiration will be extremely helpful.

It can be easy to get hung up on having to translate your inspiration literally. You might be inspired by the family pet, but instead of making a quilt with dogs or cats, maybe you design a quilt that is the

same coloring of the pet. Or you may use a favorite photo of the pet and the entire color palette comes from the photo, not just limited to the pet's coloring.

Inspiration can be how shapes and color make you feel. If you want to make a quilt that reminds you of your trip to Hawaii, use shapes and colors that recall the feelings from the trip. This was the exact inspiration for *Palm Fronds* (page 26). While the quilt design has a tropical feeling, I never saw plants in Hawaii that looked like those represented in my design. Instead, I chose to use shapes that felt tropical and a color palette that represented what I saw there— rich greens and bright hues.

The author's color plan for *Palm Fronds* (page 26)

Photo by Heather Black

Palm Fronds, 60˝ × 72˝, designed, pieced, and quilted by Heather Black

The opposite of literal is figurative, and it is possible to be so figurative or abstract that your quilt loses its relationship to your inspiration. This isn't bad, but you might want to take it into consideration when talking about your designs. I often say if it's so abstract that I need a paragraph to describe it, I probably don't have to worry about relating it back to my original inspiration. I just accept it as a design element that needs no explanation.

Sometimes the design journey is the inspiration. This can mean that not every design has a story; sometimes it is just a design you like. This doesn't make it an inferior design; it just means that you arrived at the finished impression from a different avenue.

The design journey can be the inspiration and trial and error may lead to some amazing quilts.

There will be times in your quilt design journey where there is no inspiration, when you can't come up with a design you like or want to make. At times like these, the best inspiration can be stepping away and taking a break from designing and making quilts. This can be hard to do. At times like these, I struggle with feeling that I am getting left behind by the quilting world, but that is just a feeling and not reality. Taking a break for a week or two will only benefit your quilt designing, not hurt it. In an inspiration drought, it's a good idea to not go looking for inspiration. Forcing a design isn't fulfilling and it's usually far from your best work. Taking a much-needed break will give you a fresh-new look at your quilt designing and you will be inspired again.

Inspiration can come for a myriad of things and is personal to the artist. Inspiration can be something that leaves an impression, a physical object you want to translate into a quilt, or a feeling that you want to represent in shape and color. There's no good inspiration, no bad inspiration, just inspiration. All that matter is that it inspired you to be creative.

PICK A THEME

Why Knot, 49˝ × 63˝, designed, pieced, and quilted by Heather Black

You've found your inspiration and you have a basic idea of what you'd like your design to look like. Before you jump right in, stop for a second and pick a theme. The theme can be detailed, or it can be vague. For *Why Knot* (above), I decided early on I wanted it to be playful. It was the *Why Knot* quilt and not the *Tied in Knots* quilt. Picking a theme will help guide your design, especially when you get stuck. Revisiting your theme can help you choose colors and quilting designs. A theme can help with a name for the quilt, and it can even help in the selecting of thread and backings.

Sometimes a theme comes quickly, but other times you may not know right at start of your design. Themes can be a feeling the quilt gives you, the personality of the quilt, as simple as a color temperature—for example, hot or cold—or a season. A great time to think about a theme is when you start working with the fabric. Many times, touching fabric and seeing fabrics interact with the each other in the design will lead to a theme.

The important thing is to keep the search for a theme in the forefront of your mind. Something will come to you, and you will thank yourself later when it does. I always relish the moments when a quilt design or project picks up a nickname. Nicknames make great themes and usually convey information about the design in just a word or two. For example, *Palm Fronds* (page 26) was my Hawaii quilt. Just using the nickname evoked feelings and inspiration and was used as my theme. I even used the theme when picking the quilting design.

It's a good idea to have a theme to get past some harder choices in your design. But you don't have to choose a theme with every quilt, especially if your inspiration is theme enough. After telling you how important it is to pick a theme, I am now going to tell you to not worry if you never come up with one. Sometimes quilts may be for a job deadline, quilt challenge, or charity project and don't require a theme outside the parameters given. While a theme is exceptionally helpful when you get in a design pinch, you can have a successful design without one. Think of a theme as bumpers on a dock. You don't intend to crash your boat into the dock, but when a large wave comes it's nice that they are there. You don't intend to struggle through your quilt design, but if you get stuck it's nice to have a theme to guide you to a solution. There are no hard-and-fast rules here, and if a theme is not coming to you, just move on. Chances are once you've dived into the project, a theme will come to you.

Palm Fronds stages of design

Photo by Heather Black

CREATING BALANCE

Okay, now comes the fun part—the designing! In the next few chapters I will be sharing some of my tips and tricks for creating successful quilt designs. Many of my tips have technical terms, but in staying true to how I learned design, I'm not going to worry about creating a glossary that you need to commit to memory. I'm going to focus on explaining design in a way that is approachable and understandable for all quilt designers regardless of their backgrounds.

Misprint. See the project instructions (page 119).

THREE IS YOUR FRIEND

I'm sure many of you have heard of the **rule of thirds**, which says that you should divide the surface of your artwork or into thirds, both vertically and horizontally, and put any major elements of that artwork on the dividing lines between the thirds or at the points where the lines intersect.

This term is just a fancy way of saying that layouts that are set to one side of the center or the other are more pleasing than layouts perfectly centered. For example, look how the *Misprint* design changes when the dots are moved from the left two-thirds of the quilt to the center of the quilt. The offset version of has more energy and movement and, in general, is more interesting to look at than the version with the dots centered on the aqua background. The centered dots feel stagnant and boring in comparison. This is an example of the rule of thirds.

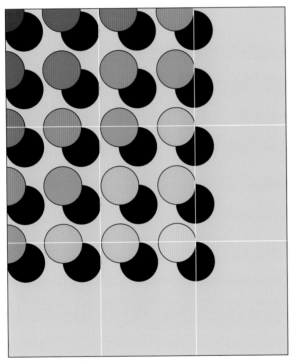

Misprint with offset dots

Misprint with centered dots

Even though this isn't a great slogan to live your life by, it is perfectly fine in art/design—*rules are made to be broken*. Most of these design tips and tricks are guidelines and not hard-and-fast rules. Design tips are intended to convey information. For example, following the rule of thirds can lead to a design that is more relaxing and casual. But if you want a design that is more structured and ordered, throw the rule of thirds out.

Another advantage of the rule of thirds is that it helps guide the viewer's eye around the quilt. If you have an accent color that you want to stand out, placing it where the rule of thirds lines intersect is a perfect way to draw attention to it.

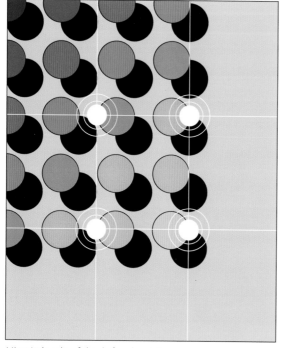

Misprint's rule of thirds focal points

Revisiting the rule of thirds is great when your design layout isn't working. Applying the rule of thirds to your quilt blocks or design elements such as color will help balance the design and it will get you past most layout difficulties. When I designed *Misprint*, I started out with the group of dots perfectly centered in the quilt. It wasn't a bad design, but I just wasn't excited about it. I changed the colors; it didn't work. Then by chance I moved the dots off the edge of the canvas, and it was magic. I aligned all the colored dots to the left two-thirds of the quilt, leaving the right third without any colored dots. The rule of thirds made all the difference in the world. It drew my eyes to the dots and at the same time added interest to the negative space, or the background. (For more details about this quilt, see the full project of *Misprint*, page 119.)

While offset layouts are generally more pleasing to look at, there are times when you may want to place a design element dead center. For example, a medallion quilt is typically completely centered and a beautiful design. Adding a design element along the vertical or horizontal center line will make it stand out, and that might be exactly what you are looking for.

The rule of thirds is a good technique to spice up a design you're are pleased with or a great guide when making a layout. Remember that design rules aren't so much a rule as a language.

ODD VERSUS EVEN

Odd-numbered groupings are considered more visually appealing than even-numbered groupings. Sometimes the grouping is obvious, such as 5 blocks instead of 6. Other times it's not as obvious, such as a color that shows up in a design 7 times instead of 8.

It's not necessary to avoid even numbers at all cost, and, frankly, it's impossible—whenever you add 2 odd numbers together, you get an even number. But when in doubt about how many elements should be in a grouping, choose an odd number.

In *Road Trip* (next page), the individual design elements in the rows are, for the most part, grouped in odds: 5 yellow circles, 7 squares in each of 2 rows, 13 white squares in each of 3 rows, and 5 green half-circles.

There are even-numbered groupings in that quilt too: 4 blue stripes on each end and 4 orange stripes; but notice the 3 sets of stripes in the quilt—tricky. I'd also like to note that this quilt was not designed with the rule of thirds in mind, and that's okay. You don't have to use every design technique for every quilt design. Design tips and tricks are useful as tools but you typically don't need a hammer and a screwdriver to hammer in a nail. It's good to pick the right tool for your design and leave some of the techniques behind.

TIP

You don't have to use every design technique for every quilt design it's good to pick the right tool for your design and leave some of the techniques behind.

Another good use of odd numbers is when your design requires the development of a repeating pattern. If you want a block, design element, or color to appear only occasionally in your design, counting off a pattern is a great way to integrate that design. For example, if you have a series of blue squares and you want to add a black square every so often, it's better to place the black square after every odd-numbered blue square instead of every even-numbered blue square. This is useful for quilting motifs too.

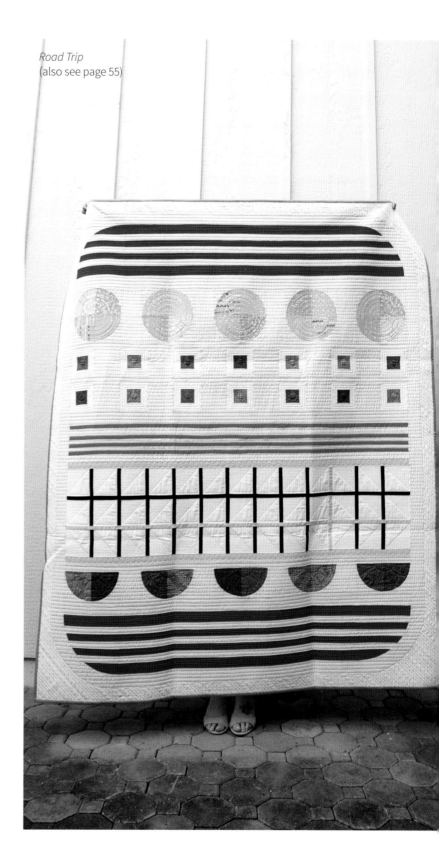

Road Trip
(also see page 55)

THE S-CURVE

I picked up this great technique in my freshman year of high school. The S-curve is a great way to add movement to a design. My ninth-grade art teacher was teaching us how to draw faces, a very interesting process for sure, and when we got to the point of adding hair to our people, she introduced the class to the S-curve. After that, I saw S-curves everywhere. When I started designing quilts, I incorporated it as a design technique for laying out blocks. An S-curve is just what it sounds like, a shape or line that mimics the curves of an S, sometimes called a *serpentine curve*.

Using an S-curve is a great way to travel from the top of a design to the bottom. In *Stratagem* (next page), I varied the size of the circles. I used the largest circle in the top right as my starting point, then carried

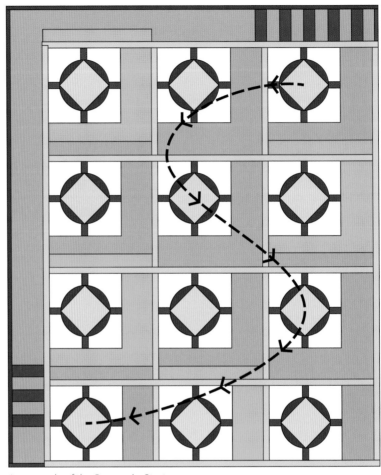

An example of the S-curve in *Stratagem*

the viewer's eye via an S-curve by following the large circles down to the bottom of the quilt. As you can see, the S doesn't need to be perfect, but it should start on one side of the design and meander back and forth down the design to the opposite side. This can be done with blocks like I did in *Stratagem* or any other design elements to create a sense of depth in your design as well to carry a person's eye throughout the quilt. S-curves are often used in paintings to make a stream or river appear to be coming out of the distance.

This is a perfect way to distribute color throughout your quilt. The S-curve works so well because it's a soft, gentle curve and a familiar-natural shape. This means if you want to add a feeling of stress or want to disconnect a part of your design from another, break a clearly defined S-curve. The viewer's eye will naturally follow the S-shape down your quilt, so breaking the movement can change a pastoral moment into a chaotic moment—which may be a better fit with your inspiration or theme. Knowing what a design technique can do is a great way to create the opposite effect by altering the technique. Just like the rule of thirds (see Three Is Your Friend, page 31) and Odd Versus Even (page 32), an S-curve tells a story without using words and the opposite story is told when the design rule is broken.

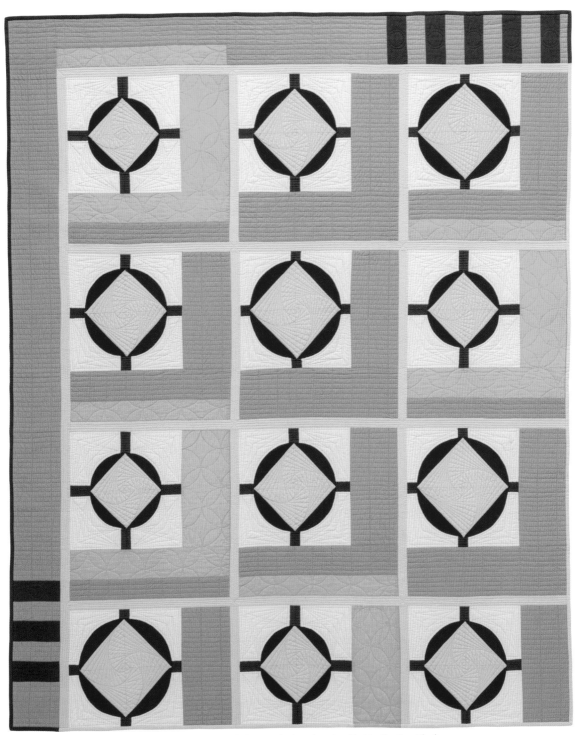

Stratagem, 60˝ × 72˝, designed, pieced, and quilted by Heather Black

RELY ON A GRID

Every quilt I design is built on a grid—every quilt, even my improv pieced quilts. Using a grid is the best way to keep balance in your design. While the tips and tricks mentioned earlier in the chapter are optional for a good design, I would argue that a grid is a necessity for a good design.

One of the most frequent mistakes I see in modern quilts is what I like to call no-purpose negative space.

Our eyes and brains are amazing, and they can pick up on details that we aren't even aware of. Have you ever looked at a quilt and initially liked it, but on second glance felt that there was something not quite right about the design or that it was unsettling for all the wrong reasons? This is probably because the negative space—the space that surrounds the subject of the design—is haphazard and not planned out. If you use a grid, this will not happen, and your design will be well balanced. Just like any other design tip and trick, if you want to convey a feeling of unbalance, work against the grid. Typically, a balanced design will be more pleasing than a design out of balance.

How does the grid work? I like to begin my designs by picking one of two quilt sizes—50″ × 60″ or 60″ × 72″. Most of the time I choose 60″ × 72″ because it's a great throw quilt size. But more importantly, 60 and 72 are divisible evenly by 2, 3,

4, 6, and 12, giving me more options for my design elements and block sizes. With that in mind, I will use a grid that has squares the size that is divisible evenly into the dimensions of the quilt. A quilt 50″ × 60″ is great for 5″ and 10″ blocks. If you know the size of blocks or units you will be using, pick a quilt size that works with that block. For example, if I know I will be designing with a 7″ block, I will adjust my quilt size to fit that block. Instead of starting at 60″ × 72″, I may start at 49″ × 63″ or 63″ × 77″. Breaking the units down further—for example, breaking a 7″ block down to 3½″—will give me a great dimension for borders and sashing.

Grounded (see the full project, page 93) is a perfect example of designing on a grid. It was designed using a 3″ grid. That means all measurements are multiples of 3—3″, 6″, 9″, and 12″. The blocks are 9″ square and are made up of units 3″ and 6″ wide. The borders are 3″ wide. All these measurements relate to each other and create balance.

If this design wasn't built on a grid, I may have had units 4″ and 5″ in width to make up my 9″ block and I may have chosen 7″ borders. The quilt would have still looked okay, but keeping everything in balance really makes the design sing. Let's take a look at an illustration that shows the grid at work. You can see from the combination of the design and grid they both fit nicely together with units having dimensions of 3″, 6″, and 9″.

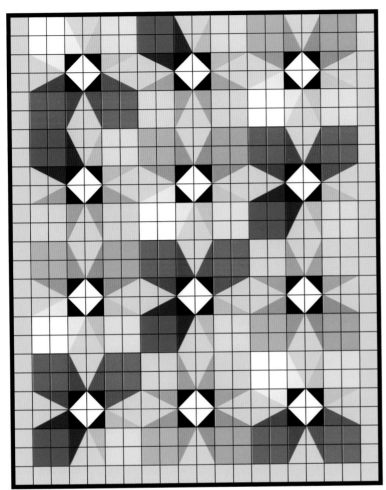

Grounded design on a grid. See the project instructions (page 93).

Hide the Grid

Using a grid as the foundation of your design makes keeping balance effortless. This is true even though it may not be a block-based design. Using a hidden grid will keep all those more complicated designs in balance.

Instead of all the blocks remaining in rows as they are in block-based designs, in a hidden grid, the blocks or design elements are spread out over the grid. All the units should have a common denominator—yes, there is math involved in this—and the negative space should fit in the grid as well.

Using a hidden grid is a bit more complicated than a non-hidden grid. See *Around Town*, also one of the projects (full project, page 107, and full quilt photo, page 116). You can make the quilt and get some hands-on experience making a quilt with a hidden grid. While designing *Around Town*, I used a 3″ grid. All the design elements—the half-circles, squares, rectangles, background shapes, and stripes—are sized as multiples of 3. Even though there is very little tying the different blocks and design elements together, they all relate to each other because of the hidden grid. Without any effort, there is balance in the design. The balance in *Around Town* would have been more difficult to accomplish without a hidden grid. More likely than not, the design would have been out of balance and not as pleasing or calming.

Using a grid in block-based designs or in a hidden grid design is essential to a visually pleasing quilt. There are other benefits to using a grid and I will discuss later in the book how using a grid will help in the actual making of the quilt. You don't have to use my sizes to use a grid. Sometimes you know what block you want to use, so the grid is set for you, and other times you start out with a quilt size that ends up changing as you continue to design. No matter what size quilt you are making or how you get to that size, always remember to use a grid.

Around Town on a grid. See the project instructions (page 107).

STABILIZE THE DESIGN

Borders are more common in traditional quilts rather than modern quilts. Though many modern quilts do not have borders, they can be an integral part of a modern quilt. When I make a block-based design, I often add a border and have the background of the blocks bleed over into the borders of the design, so it looks like they are floating on top of the background.

Grounded. See the project instructions (page 93).

You can see this in *Grounded*. The colored blocks are sitting on top of the light aqua background. When I began designing this quilt, I started with the blocks centered on the background with an equal-width border all around the body of the quilt. This design looked okay, but there was something unsettling about the blocks floating on a sea of aqua. That's when I decided that I needed to stabilize the design or set it on a base. I eliminated the top border to create a base for my blocks to stand on.

This design trick is a great way to add a calming feeling to your designs. Much like an upside-down pyramid, an object with a smaller bottom than top is translated in our minds as unsteady. Adding a base to your quilts is a good way to stabilize the design. If your quilt design is feeling a bit top heavy, adding a wider bottom border can help counter the top-heavy effect.

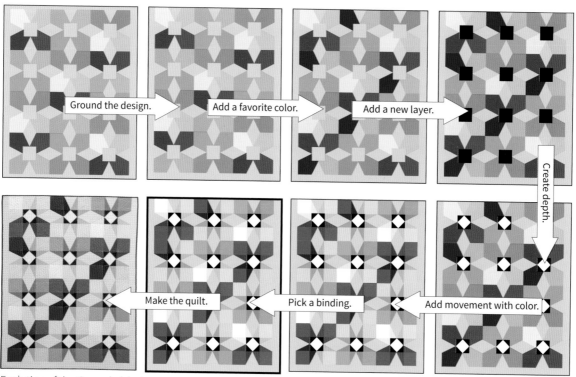

Evolution of the *Grounded* design

Adding a base to your design doesn't mean you always have to eliminate the top border all together. *Sunset Horizons* (next page), a quilt from my first book with coauthor Daisy Aschehoug, *Quilt Modern Curves & Bold Stripes* (page 127), still has a top border; it's just smaller than the bottom border. This has the same effect of stabilizing the design.

Even though the two borders are different sizes, they are still sized according to the grid. For example, the top, right, and left borders may be 6″ wide while the bottom border is 9″ wide to maintain the balance while stabilizing the design.

Next time you have a design, especially a block-based design, that's starting to feel a little off kilter, stabilize it with a larger bottom border. This tip is a great easy fix and is an easy way to add a modern touch to a block based design.

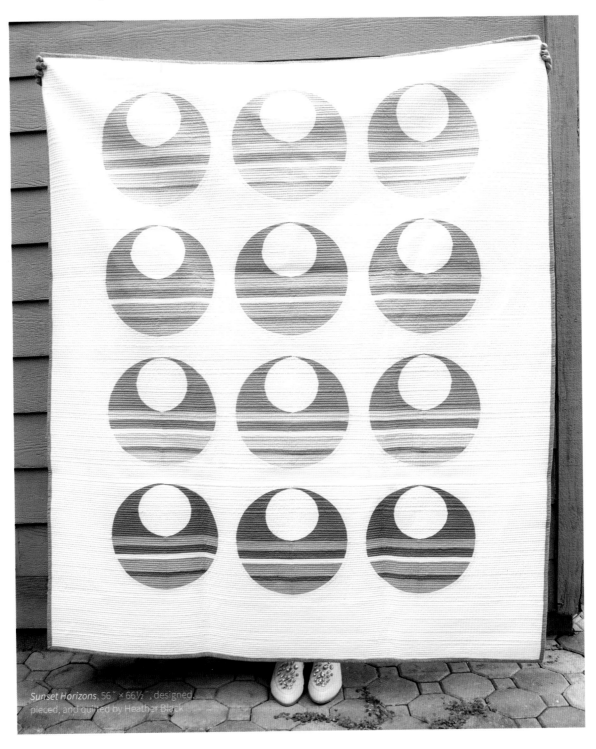

Sunset Horizons, 56˝ × 66½˝, designed, pieced, and quilted by Heather Black

USING DESIGN TO TELL A STORY

Make your designs tell a story. Just as a picture is worth 1,000 words, where you place design elements in your quilt will convey information to the viewer. There are a few tips and tricks you can use to give your designs movements and depth just by changing a few elements of your design. In this chapter, I will be referencing *Moving Through* (page 100), which also is a sample project.

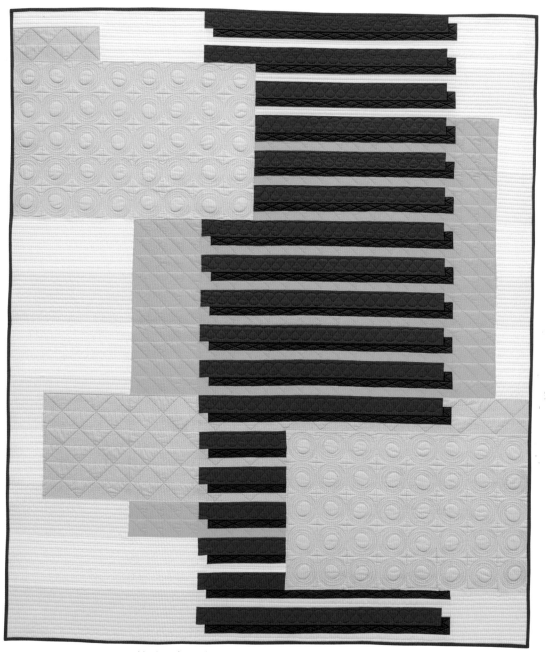

Moving Through. See the project instructions (page 100).

MOVEMENT

We've already touched on one of the ways to create movement in your designs, the S-curve, but there are other ways to create movement. The quickest way to add movement to any design is to add stripes to the design, either pieced or a printed. When you look at *Moving Through*, it has plenty of motion, but what gets all the different elements going is the subtly striped pink and white background. Horizontal stripes have a calm feeling and vertical lines communicate more energy. The highest-energy stripes are set on an angle. This is why many optical illusions use stripes; our brains naturally associate them with movement. This is true of your quilt layout as well. A traditional layout in rows will have less energy than a columnar layout and both have less energy than a quilt laid out on point.

Movement can also be created by design elements "passing" from one side of the quilt surface to another. In *Moving Through*, the lavender and blue rectangles are doing just that. At the top, they look as if they are traveling from left to right and at the bottom, they appear to be traveling from right to left. This works because design elements with a large, empty space to one side or the other will appear as if they are moving into that empty space, meaning an area not containing the identical design element. In addition, objects closer to each other will look as if they are traveling faster than objects farther apart in the same quilt, as long as there is an empty space they are "moving" into. This is one of the ways to tell a story with movement. Using the placement of a design element can help your quilt communicate to the viewer without words.

Just as placing design elements on the right or left side makes it look as if they are passing from one edge of the quilt to another, placing objects on one end of the quilt or the other can give the impression that they are moving up or down the surface of the quilt. On *Moving Through*, because the blue stripes are touching the top, they appear to be moving from the top of the quilt to the bottom. If I had left the space at the top and had a blue stripe touching the bottom, the stripes would have appeared to be coming up for the bottom of the quilt. This is because objects will appear to be moving into an empty area on the quilt. Again, the quilt can communicate a feeling or movement without words.

Close-up of Moving Through

DEPTH

One of the most useful design tips I learned while watching Bob Ross's *Joy of Painting* was something that is fairly obvious but elusive if you don't stop to think about it. Painting is, for the most part, the illusion of making a two-dimensional object look three-dimensional. Being pretty young when I heard that, I really didn't get what he was saying. I thought of a cube or a sphere or even blue and red 3-D glasses. But when I recalled that statement as an adult, I began to look for design tips and tricks for making an object look three-dimensional or for learning what gives an object depth. A quilt has length and width, but an interesting design will create depth on the two-dimensional quilt canvas.

If you are trying to tell a story with a quilt that involves unique planes and layers, try making the two-dimensional design elements look three-dimensional.

An object will look three-dimensional because of the shadow it casts. Long shadows occur when the sun is lower near the horizon; when the sun is directly overhead, shadows will almost disappear. Being aware of this and applying it to your quilt design will tell a story about the time your design is set in.

In *Moving Through* (page 42), not only are the rectangles and stripes moving over the surface of the quilt, they are also layered on top of each other. The blue stripes are even casting a shadow on the layers beneath them. Creating the illusion of layers will add depth to your design. Not only will the viewer's eye move from top to bottom and left to right, it will also move from near to far, all on a two-dimensional surface. You also can enhance the depth of your design with quilting choices (see Finish the Design with Quilting, page 63).

COLOR

This will be probably be the design element you have the most experience with. Colors can quickly communicate a story in your design. We even refer to colors in terms that instantly tell you about them—color stories, cool palette, warm palette. I will go more in-depth into colors in Designing with Color (page 46), but for now it's important to remember that colors can work with the story or they can work against it.

If you are trying to make a quilt inspired by a day in the desert, you probably wouldn't want to use an icy blue. Conversely, inspiration from a crisp winter walk probably won't include an over-abundance of mango orange. I'm not saying you wouldn't want to include those colors at all, but the overall color of your design will match the inspiration or theme. Another example, if you were making a cheerful quilt you won't want to use only black, gray and brown. There are cases when you are trying to create

Detail of *Grounded* (page 39)

conflict in your design so it can be useful to pick a color palette in opposition to your inspiration or theme. For example, if you want one section or element in your "cheery" quilt to represent sorrow, try choosing a different color palette for that section.

Color is the fastest way to communicate your desired story.

Colors evoke emotion. Using those traditional color emotions in a different way than expected will communicate stress or chaos. Challenging the conventional thinking is one way to draw the desired emotion out of the viewer.

Using both placement and color is a great way to communicate details about the inspiration and theme of your quilt design. Being aware of what these elements are saying and how they affect the design can prevent frustration during the design process. Choose elements that complement what you are trying to say and your design will speak for you.

DESIGN ELEMENT	THE STORY IT TELLS
Horizontal lines	Calm, pastoral, arcadian, low-key, harmonious
Vertical lines	Active, wired, intent, alert, vigor, ready
Angled lines	Energetic, dynamic, zippy, charismatic, lively
Morning/evening shadows	Long, beginning, ending, cool, calming
Midday shadows	Small, high energy, warm, exciting
Planes	Depth, prominence, mystery, furtive, surreptitious
Cool colors	Cold, sadness, winter, calming, contentment, soothing
Warm colors	Hot, angry, summer, energizing, agitated, restless

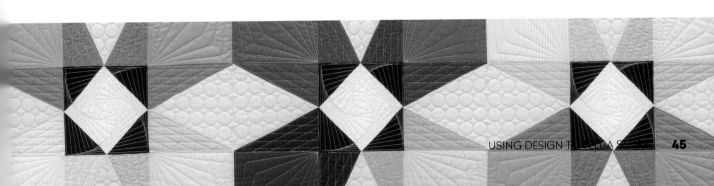

DESIGNING
with COLOR

Color wheel
Photo by Heather Black

CHOOSING COLORS

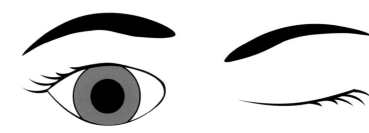

Visible Light Spectrum

| Radio | Micro Waves | Infrared | ROYGBIV | Ultra Violet | X-Ray | Gamma Ray |

ELECTROMAGNETIC WAVE SPECTRUM

For years when I heard the term "color theory," my mind would freeze, and I'd get the sinking feeling that knowing how to apply colors to my quilt designs had suddenly become impossible. When people talk about color theory, it can be intimidating. In actuality, they aren't even explaining true color theory. Real color theory is something I learned in chemistry.

In simple terms, when an electromagnetic wave is absorbed by an atom or molecule it excites the electrons to a higher orbital but since that orbital is an unstable state for the electron, it moves back down to its original orbital. When the electron returns to its original orbital, it releases energy in the form of an electromagnetic wave, minus the energy it took to move to the higher orbital, and if it is within the visible light spectrum, we see it as color. That's what I think color theory is and, *thankfully*, it has nothing to do with designing quilts. That is why I'm not going to teach "color theory" when it comes to designing quilts. Throw that term away. I am going to discuss the basics of how colors interact with each other followed by how it works in design. This is quilt making, not chemistry, after all.

Hi, I'm Atom Man. . . .

Illustrations by Heather Black

THE BASICS

Color isn't complicated. It's all around us every day. We are surrounded by color. Much of what we know about color we learned in elementary school, but a quick refresher will get you thinking about colors on a simple color wheel. There are three primary colors: red, yellow, and blue. These colors cannot be created by mixing other colors together. Secondary colors are colors that are made by mixing two primary colors together: orange, green, and purple or violet. Finally, there are six tertiary colors. These are made by mixing a primary color with an adjacent secondary color. These twelve colors make up a very basic color wheel.

Color wheel

Illustration by Heather Black

Now that our colors are snuggly on the color wheel, we can start seeing the relationship one color has to another.

First let's look at opposites. For each primary color there is an opposite secondary color—red and green, orange and blue, and purple and yellow.

I remembered these pairs as Christmas, sunset and Easter, respectively. Opposite colors have some really interesting characteristics. They are the most dynamic, high-contrast pairings of color. More exciting, when you mix two opposite colors together, you get a hue of brown. This is particularly useful in quilt design because it will help you select a neutral for you project. These browns can be warm or cool, and depending on the look you're are going for you can pick your neutral is the same way. Do I want a warm neutral, cool neutral, or something between? Your inspiration and the colors in your design will help you decide. A brown created using orange and blue will be warm when more orange is present and cool if there is more blue. A brown with more orange might not be the right choice for a neutral when the rest of the colors in the quilt are cool. When you add white to these browns, you get tans and creams. These colors are often called *neutrals*. Neutrals are colors that do not appear on the color wheel. Brown is not present on the color wheel. Off-whites and creams are browns with white added to them.

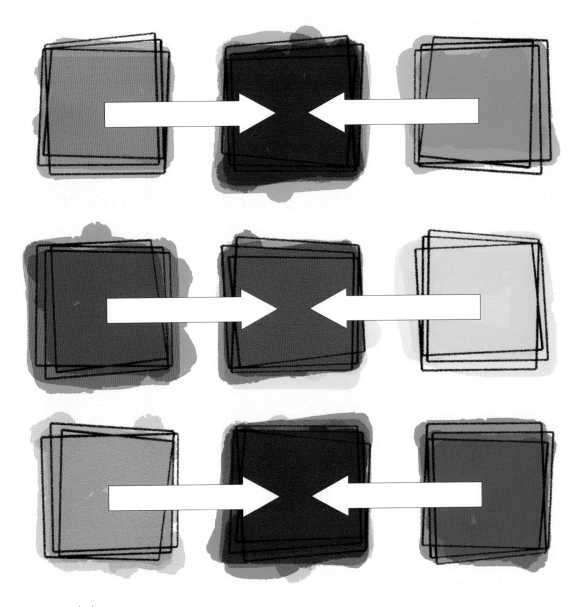

Opposites make brown.

Illustration by Heather Black

Here are a few more color terms that will help you in choosing fabric colors for your quilt design.

- **Warm colors** are typically colors found on the red, orange, and yellow half of the color wheel.
- **Cool colors** are typically colors found on the blue, green, and purple half of the color wheel.

I say warm and cool colors are "typically" x, y, and z, because almost any color can be warm or cool. It will depend what color they are next to or where the live in the spectrum for that color. Think of a purple that is more red than blue; it will come across as warm color even though I listed purple as "typically" a cool color. I like to think of this as color relativity.

For example, my mom remodeled her kitchen several years back and she picked out some beautiful cream cabinets. She asked my sister in law and me to help her pick a paint color for the kitchen. As we started to hold swatches up to the cabinets, anything with a hint of green made the cream cabinets appear pink. I knew my mom did not want a pink kitchen, so we went with a paint that was a warmer taupe and the cabinets turned back to cream. Did the cabinets actually change colors? Well, no, but the greener colors made the reds in the cream stand out and the taupe kept the red from showing. This same concept applies to color we pick for our neutrals in our quilt designs.

Even though I started the chapter by stating I did not want to talk about color theory, I do think it is important that we are all speaking the same language when it comes to color. So it is important to go over some very basic terms. When you hear someone talking about *hue*, they are referring to a color. For example, red is a hue. Hue and color are often interchangeable.

You can manipulate hues, and one of the ways to do that is to add black or white to the hue. Adding black makes a *shade* and adding white makes a *tint* of that hue. For example, navy is a shade of blue and pink is a tint of red. Knowing how black and white affect colors will help when designing quilts, especially ombré designs.

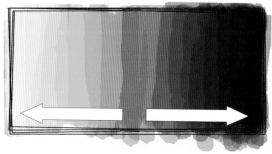

Tint and shade

Illustration by Heather Black

Another aspect of color that quilt designers like to see is the saturation of the fabric. *Saturation* refers to the intensity of the color. If a color is very opaque, it will appear more saturated. As the transparency of that color is diluted, it will look less opaque. A less-saturated color allows more of the background to show through. Typically with fabric, less-saturated colors will let more of the white, off-white, or cream of the undyed base fabric show through. In paints, in most cases an unsaturated color will fade to gray.

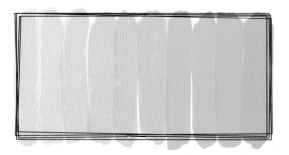

Saturation

Illustration by Heather Black

Finally, I want to touch on value. Discussing value has been a very popular topic among quilters and quilt designers. There are ways to see value in your designs from taking black and white pictures to wearing special glasses, but adding value to your designs doesn't have to be complicated. *Value* is how light or dark a color is and is tied closely to shades, tints, and saturation. Remember the balloon tip I overheard as a preteen? One of the reasons the customer was able to combine any three balloon colors and they would go together is because all the balloons had the same value. The balloons were also made of the same material, so as they were blown up, they would all have the same saturation. It is good to know what values you are using in your designs. Varying value in your quilt will add depth and interest with minimal work. Below is a color palette with varying values. The hues are different, but the values of those hues also vary.

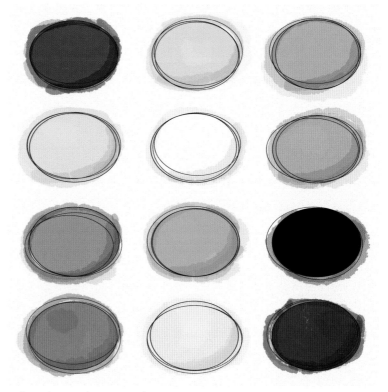

Color palette with varying values

Illustration by Heather Black

While varying the value is very useful and part of creating a pleasing color palette, it isn't absolutely necessary. Many pieces of art, especially modern art, do not have different values in them. For example, Bauhaus art pieces use a limited color palette, sometimes featuring only primary colors. These designs do not vary in value and yet are outstanding works of art.

I truly believe the above is more than you need to know to work with colors in your designs, but it is useful to understand and to properly use color terms when discussing your designs with others. It is easier to learn from each other when we are all speaking the same language.

EXPERIMENT WITH COLOR

By far the best way to learn about color is to use color. Trial and error can be tedious, but it can also be educational. That's why I want to encourage you to buy a watercolor set, make sure it includes white paint, and start playing with colors. A good place to start are the definitions we just went over. Test them out, see if I'm right. Do you really get brown when you mix equal parts of opposite colors? Can you really make a purple look like a warm color by placing it near other colors? If you are looking to do something more sophisticated, play with tints and shade by drawing a rectangle and separating it into 11 columns. Paint the far-left column white and the far-right column black. In the center column, paint your favorite hue/color, then gradate it from the center on the left side all the way to white and on the right side all the way to black. Experiment with saturation. Add more and more water to a color and see how diluting the paint changes the saturation. Finally, paint your favorite quilt and see how those colors can be reproduced with the watercolors.

These are quick exercises that you can do to hone your color skills. Knowing how colors interact with white, black, gray and other colors will help you in picking color palettes for your quilt designs.

Swatches in watercolor

Photo by Heather Black

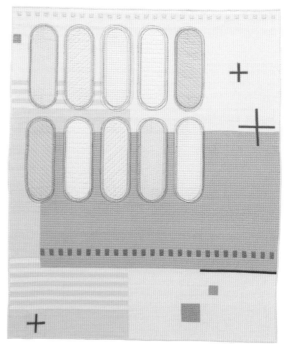

Swatches, 60″ × 72″, designed pieced, and quilted by Heather Black

Watercolor set

Photo by Heather Black

NATURE DOESN'T CARE ABOUT COLOR THEORY

Sometimes it can be difficult to choose a complete color palette when designing quilts. If you are feeling stuck or if you can't figure out where to start, turn to nature for inspiration. You can take a look around you or find unlimited pictures of nature online. There are even websites and phone apps that focus solely on creating color palettes from pictures of nature.

From sunsets to exotic animals, the world is full of beautiful colors. From a complex coral reef to the simplicity of a desert landscape there are always places to find color inspiration in nature. The color inspiration for *Bird Watching* was a photo of a Bohemian waxwing. I stayed true to the colors of the waxwing, but I didn't restrict myself to only the colors of the bird—tans, black, white, yellow, and red. I also added blue and pink to complement the color palette. The best thing of all, nature doesn't care about color theory, yet the color palettes are beautiful.

Bohemian waxwing

Photo by Martin Mecnarowski / Shutterstock.com

Bird Watching, 40˝ × 48˝, designed, pieced, and quilted by Heather Black

CREATE YOUR OWN COLOR THEORY

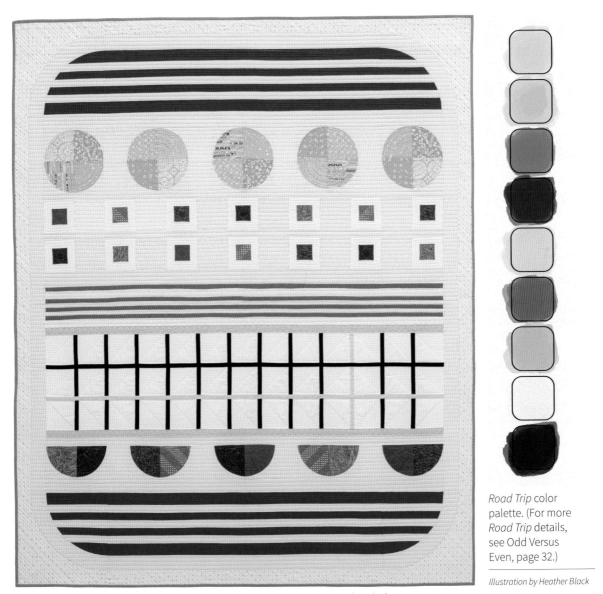

Road Trip color palette. (For more *Road Trip* details, see Odd Versus Even, page 32.)

Illustration by Heather Black

Road Trip, 60″ × 72″, designed, pieced, and quilted by Heather Black

Finding inspiration from photography or nature is good, especially when you are struggling with what colors to use. But what is even more exciting is creating your own color palette. One of the reasons I reject the idea of there being a color theory for design is it makes it sound as if you could produce perfect color combinations all the time as long as you know all about the "science" of color. This is simply not true.

THE PERFECT PALETTE?

There is no such thing as the perfect color palette because colors are subjective. Sure, each electromagnetic wave of visible light has its own unique wavelength, but the way people translate those wave lengths from our eyes to our brain is subjective. My dad is color-blind. He's never been able to see subtle differences between blue, green, and brown. He can see the difference between royal blue and kelly green, but all the colors between get a little murky for him. Even if I found a color palette I could call perfect, he wouldn't see it the same as I do. There is no perfect color palette standard you have to live up to, and no person can make a universally liked color palette. You may love how a fellow quilter uses color in their designs and think they have a special command over color, but more likely you like the same colors as that quilter and that is what you admire about their palette. Someone with different tastes may not care for the colors used in their designs and may even think they don't know how to use color. Color is subjective.

The secret to a perfect color palette is to design with colors you like! Ever since we learned to talk, people have been asking us what our favorite color is. If you're my daughter, the answer is, "Rainbow!" If you have trouble deciding, look at your wardrobe. Is there a color that stands out? Is there a color that is absent? You can do the same thing with your home decor. I have very few cool colors in my home. Most are pinks, orange, and warm neutrals. I can also say that the majority of my wardrobe has fall colors, again not too many cool blues and greens. We all have colors we like and colors we don't care for. Designing with colors you like will lead to more successful designs and designs you are more likely to create a quilt from.

LOOK AT THE THEME

I hope you took a moment to think over some of your favorite colors and have a good understanding of your likes and dislike, but how do you make a palette from those colors? This is where having a theme for your design can come in handy. When you begin to assemble a palette, it's more important to communicate an overall impression than to focus on the individual colors in the palette. When I made *Why Knot* (page 28), I knew I wanted something with whimsy, so I picked bright, very bright, colors for the palette and introduced a black-and-white stripe for movement and playfulness. Color palettes can communicate instantly with the viewer. If you want to design a moody quilt, don't pick bright sunny colors. Remember that colors communicate just as effectively as words. Someone's language, culture, and experiences will define the meanings of color, so be familiar with what the colors in your design are saying to you.

Why Knot watercolor painting

Photo by Heather Black

CREATING INTEREST IN THE PALETTE

It isn't necessary to vary values—the lightness and darkness—of the colors in your palette unless it is your design goal. Interest in a color palette can be created in several different ways. High-contrast palettes, those containing colors opposite each other on the color wheel, are one way to create interest that doesn't necessarily mean the values vary. What is most important is to use colors you like. If you don't like pastels, don't force yourself to use them, even if that means all the colors in your palette are the same value. In *Around Town* (see full project, page 107), all the background colors have a light value, but the featured colors are all a darker value. This is the same for *Moving Through* (page 100). Only *Grounded* (page 93) uses a color palette that consistently varies the values in the palette. What unifies each of these color palettes is that they focus on a design goal and stay true to their theme.

Close-up of *Around Town*. See the project instructions (page 107).

COLOR WORKS

I love letting color do all the hard work for me in my designs. Color can create movement, add depth, and direct the viewer's eye.

One of the most useful design tools I've used is that warm colors will appear to be hovering over the quilt background if the background is a cool color and, conversely, cool colors will appear to sink into a warm-colored background. A great example of this technique in action is *Misprint* (below; full project, page 119). The warm reds and oranges look like they are bouncing off the background while the shadows appear to be sinking into the background. This is an excellent example of color relativity. The aqua background acts as a cool color when paired with the warm reds, oranges, and yellows but feels warm when placed with the cool navy blue of the shadows.

Misprint. See the project instructions (page 119).

If you want your design to appear to have several planes, consider using warm and cool colors to create that multilayer effect. Conversely, if you want your quilt to be all on the same plane or two, don't place warm colors on a cool background or vice versa. Using warm and cool colors to create depth will simplify the piecing process. Instead of having to piece unique angles and Y-seams to create planes in your design, let the colors do the heavy lifting to achieve the same look.

To make an object that is two-dimensional look as if it is three-dimensional, you need to add a shadow. Shadows can be completely different colors than the main object or they can be a darker shade of the same hue. If you look at where the blocks come together in *Grounded* (page 93), they have a square with two sides that are shadows. It gives the impression that you are looking down at a tall building. In this design, the shadows are

similar in color to the top square, but it still has the effect of making the object look three-dimensional.

Adding dimension to your design is similar to adding planes. To avoid difficult piecing, consider using color instead. When it comes time to add shadows to your design, it will help to know how colors react to the influence of gray or black. Here's where taking the time to play with watercolors will pay off in your design. While the simplest shadow is a black or gray, a shadow can also be achieved by using a shade of the color. Observing shadows in real life will benefit your designs as well. Keep shading all on one side to mimic a light source or create a look where the shadow gradually gets darker to create depth. These are things that we may subconsciously know but if you don't stop and take note, it may impact your design in a way you don't like.

Close-up of *Grounded*, which looks three-dimensional. See project instructions (page 93).

Transparency is similar to shadowing but instead of just adding black, or making the hue darker, you take into consideration what color will be behind the color you are trying to make transparent. If you are designing overlapping squares and one is blue and the other is red, the area where they overlap will be purple. The mixing of the two colors is what creates the illusion that the fabrics are transparent. In *The Cool Kids*, I created the look of transparency where the white and black circles of equal saturation overlap, making a medium gray.

The Cool Kids, 50″ × 60″, designed, pieced, and quilted by Heather Black

Again, actually knowing how colors interact with each other will help you accomplish a successful transparency in your quilt design. If you don't know what happens when pink is mixed with aqua, you won't be able to choose a color for the transparency. If you have a design software like Photoshop or Illustrator, you can play with colors in the software. By changing the transparency or layer-blending mode of an object, you can mix colors. Make a pink square and change the blending mode of the layer, then make an aqua square and change the blending mode of the layer to the same as the pink. Place one square on top of the other and see what happens. In this case, the two colors create a violet. If you were making a transparency quilt using these colors, adding a different color than violet where the blocks overlap would diminish the effect of the transparency.

Playing with transparency on the computer

Illustration by Heather Black

When you look at paintings from the Renaissance era, they look almost lifelike. Part of the reason painters were able to accomplish this is that they took into consideration atmospheric particles, moisture, and dust in the air. Objects further away don't look as saturated as objects up close. Think of a humid day and the haze that appears as you look out to the horizon. This haze lets your brain know that the less-saturated objects are farther away because they are more muted than the object closer and less obscured by the haze or humidity. I live in a very arid part of the country, and we have very few truly humid days in the year. This doesn't mean that there is no atmospheric interference. There is dust and, in the summer, frequently smoke. These particles have the same effect on how we perceive distance.

You can use this theory to create depth using color in your quilt designs. In *Around Town* (page 107), the backgrounds are not only lighter than the colors in the foreground, they are also muddier, or mixed with gray, to account for those miscellaneous particles in the air. This adds even more depth to the design.

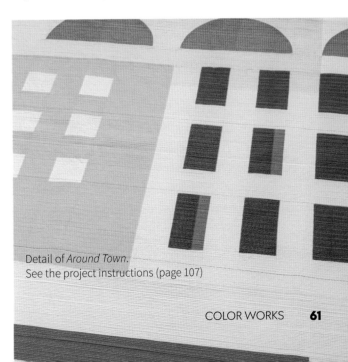

Detail of *Around Town*.
See the project instructions (page 107)

Playing with tints and saturation of colors will help you apply this concept to your designs. If you want a part of a quilt block to stand out more than another, consider muddying the background colors in the block or the sections of the block you don't want to stand out. Think of a classic Churn Dash block. If all the units are the exact same tint/shade and saturation, the positive space will stand out from the background as a single unit. If you want the half-square triangles to stand out, muddy the rectangles or vice versa.

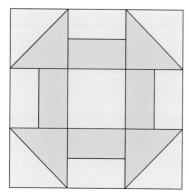

Uniform Churn Dash block

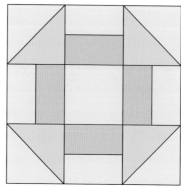

Churn Dash block with half-square triangles highlighted

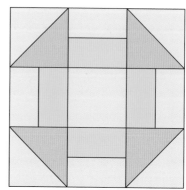

Churn Dash block with rectangles highlighted

Again, don't forget to break the rules whenever you want. These color tips and tricks are meant to help you when you get frustrated or don't know how to accomplish our design goal.

If you're faced with staying true to your design or keeping a color tip and trick, ditch the color tip. Good design comes down to whether you think it looks good. Be in control of your design and don't let these color parameters make the decisions for you. Remember to tell a story and pick a theme. When you get stuck or don't know why your design doesn't feel right or isn't working, go back to these color tips and tricks and remember how colors interact with each other. You may have a color combo in your design that is forcing an effect you didn't want.

Breaking the rules is a design choice in itself. If you want to convey stress, chaos, disorder or, on a more positive note, create a fantasy world, break the design rules. Understanding how colors interact with each other and how they create design effects will keep you from making decisions that counteract where you want the design to go.

FINISH THE DESIGN
with QUILTING

QUILTING DESIGN

Quilting your design can be scary. The first question to ask is, who is going to do the quilting. Are you going to do the quilting or are you going to send the top out to a quilter? No matter how you answer that question, it will be important to know how you want the quilting to interact with your quilt design.

If you are sending your top out for quilting, *don't* skip this chapter. Evaluating your quilt design and sharing your quilting goals with your quilter is just as important as quilting your design yourself. Giving your quilter notes on what you want to show off and what you want to fade into the background will be very helpful, and you will be more pleased with the finished quilt. Even if you are picking an allover or edge-to-edge design, taking the time to narrow down your likes and dislikes will make picking your design easier.

TAKE INVENTORY

Just as with designing your quilt, you need to take inventory of your quilting tools of the trade. Do you send your quilts out to a quilter? Do you quilt them yourself on a domestic machine, longarm, or by hand? Each of these quilting techniques require different tools and accessories. Don't plan quilting that isn't practical or possible for your quilter's tools or your tools.

In one of my first modern quilts, I wanted to quilt 2″ circles with my walking foot. This was nearly impossible to do without making the circle look more like an irregular rock formation. I was frustrated, but then I remembered I know how to hand quilt; that's what I did and it looked really good. If I had stopped and inventoried what my tools were capable of, I could have avoided all that frustration. Likewise, if you are asking your quilter to do

Trellis, 46″ × 56″, designed and quilted by Heather Black

something that he or she can't do with their tools, you are setting them up for failure. A simple example of this is quilting diagonal lines. While this is possible to do on a longarm, it is not an easy task and many longarmers will not quilt diagonal lines from one corner to the other corner without a break. On the other hand, using a domestic machine to quilt from one corner of a quilt to another is fairly simple. Knowing this beforehand, you can strategize a similar look that is easily accomplished on a longarm before you send it out to your quilter. While this seems like common sense, if you don't stop to consider the tools being used, you may get into a quilting design that is not possible or extremely frustrating.

Quilting Skills Worksheet

_____

_____

_____

_____

_____

_____

_____

_____

The second most important tool to get familiar with is your thread. Thread comes in different weights and there are several high-quality brands on the market. By far my favorite is Aurifil. I use a 50-weight for piecing. For quilting I will vary my thread weight depending on how I am quilting. When I'm hand quilting, I'll use a 12- or 28-weight Aurifil thread. On my domestic machine I quilt with 40-weight Aurifil thread, and with my longarm I quilt with Aurifil 40-weight three-ply, also called Forty3 thread. Using the wrong thread can lead to breakages and the stitches may not have the look you're looking for. The three-ply thread is a bit thicker and stronger than a typical two-ply thread. A three-ply thread is much more able to withstand the tension and forces placed on your thread when quilting straight lines on your longarm. If quilting on a domestic machine, a two-ply 50-weight or 40-weight thread will work great for most quilting designs.

It is also important to be aware of the kind and weight of thread if you are sending your quilt out to be quilted. If your quilter is going to use a lighter-weight thread when you wanted the stitches to show up, it will be good to communicate that to them before they begin quilting. Discussing the thread with your quilter will help both of you better understand what you want. Longarm quilters are a great resource for thread knowledge. They see a lot of quilts. They will know what threads blend well and they will know if your goals are even possible with your quilt. They may tell you that your design sounds amazing, but the thread and stitches won't show up on the fabrics you chose.

While the thread and quilting designs you choose are very project specific, there are some general tips for choosing thread.

- If your quilt design has a high-contrast color palette with no good blending thread option, default to a lighter thread color. In general, a lighter thread will look better on a dark fabric than a dark thread will look on a lighter fabric.

- Threads that match the fabric color exactly will camouflage mistakes much more than threads that are in high contrast to the fabric color.

- Try a neutral tan or taupe as a blending thread instead of picking an exact color match. Many times a thread color will surprise you and blend across several different fabrics.

While thread seems like an inconsequential detail, it can make the difference between an okay quilting design and a fabulous quilt design. Taking a moment to figure out your thread choice will prevent frustration and unpicking down the road. If you're sending your quilt out for quilting, your quilter will appreciate that you took the time to think through what you want.

Aurifil's Forty3 thread

Photo by Heather Black

TESTING QUILTING DESIGNS

There are a few ways to test out quilting designs without having to jump in and quilt something you'll end up taking out later. Almost no one enjoys unpicking quilting. A great low-tech way to test out quilting designs is to buy a plastic sheet protector to place your quilt design in and a dry erase marker to write on the sheet protector. This allows you to try out quilting designs with ease. Another low-tech option is to make a copy or print out a copy of your quilt design, grab your ruler, pencil, and eraser, and draw the design directly on the paper. Even though changing quilting designs isn't as easy using this technique, it is great for testing out straight lines and smaller quilting designs. Even though I design my quilts in Photoshop, I'll still print out a copy of my quilt design and test out quilting design options this way.

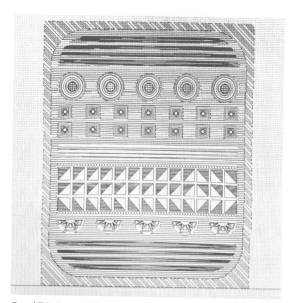

Road Trip (page 55) digital quilting design

Photo by Heather Black

In a world of the latest and greatest, there are always high-tech options for testing out quilting designs. You can test out designs in most designing software by importing an image of the quilt and using the design software to draw quilting lines over it. If you have a computerized longarm you can design your quilting using the software your longarm came with. I frequently design with my longarm design software. Sometimes I design as I go, sometimes I design off of my quilting sketches. Using a computer is a great way to resize your image to design quilting area by area in more detail. You can't do that with a low-tech option.

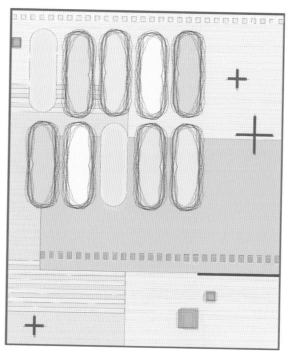

Close-up of the *Swatches* drawing, where I sketched in the quilting design. See the quilt (page 52).

Illustration by Heather Black

Whether you pick a low-tech or high-tech way to test out quilting designs, the important thing is to test the quilting design first. It's easier to erase or hit the delete button than it is to unpick quilting.

Why Knot

49x63

INVENTORY YOUR LIKES AND DISLIKES

Just like when I had you inventory your likes and dislikes when quilt designing and with colors (page 46), it is important to know what you like and dislike when choosing quilting. If you don't like straight lines, don't use them. If you don't like feathers, don't design feathers. The goal is to design quilting that you like and that will enhance your quilt design. Knowing your likes and dislikes can help you pick a quilter and better communicate with them what you want the quilting to look like.

Also, knowing your skill level will come in handy because no matter how much you like the look of ribbon candy, you won't like it if you can't execute it to look the way you want. This doesn't mean that you never try ribbon candy, but your favorite quilt top won't be the best time to experiment.

Growing your quilting skills is another place where quilt patterns come in handy. You can get a pattern that will work well with whatever quilting design you are practicing. To experiment on a domestic machine or with hand quilting, I like making a mini quilt sandwich using 10″ squares of fabric and practicing on those. On my longarm, I will add a strip of fabric at the end of a quilt and try out a new design or some free-motion quilting before unloading the quilt.

Quilting Likes and Dislikes Worksheet

Likes:

_____

_____

_____

_____

_____

Dislikes:

_____

_____

_____

_____

_____

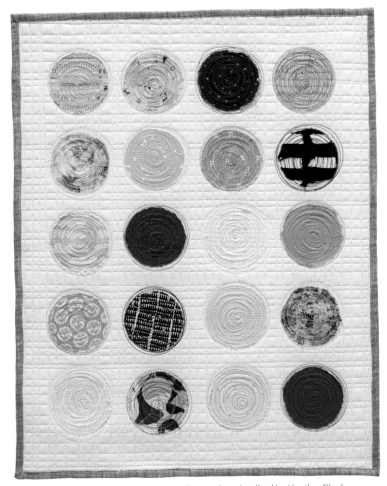

Make It Nine, 20″ × 24″, designed, pieced, and quilted by Heather Black

START EARLY

Choosing quilting designs can seem daunting. One way to make it more manageable is to start thinking about your quilting early. When you design your quilt, stop and think about what kind of quilting, you'd like to use. When you're piecing the top and you come across a fabric or section of the quilt you really like, make note of it and start thinking of what kind of quilting would highlight that area. If you've seen quilting that you've really liked in the past, try to see how a version of that quilting would work in your design.

Another way to get going on the quilting design early is to start thinking of the quilting that will work with the theme you've picked for the design. This is especially useful when you've decided to custom quilt your design, either personally or by a longarm quilter. Knowing your design can be *simple*, such as quilting a honeycomb on a bee quilt, or *thematic*, such as adding chaos to a quilt depicting disorder.

COMPLEMENT THE DESIGN

Quilting has two purposes: the first is to hold the layers of the quilt together, and the second is to make the quilt look better. This is true whether you stitch only in-the-ditch or quilt the design to death. No one wants to add quilting to a great quilt design only to make it look less impressive. I'm not talking about what your skill level when I refer to making a design look less impressive, but rather to how the quilting designs affects the overall look of the quilt. This is where knowing what parts of your quilt you want to highlight comes in handy. Typically, an area with less quilting in it will stand out more than an area with an abundance of quilting. If you don't know what you want to stand out, pick your favorite part of the quilt and start designing from there.

TIP
Typically, an area with less quilting in it will stand out more than an area with an abundance of quilting.

There are no hard-and-fast rules when it comes to quilting design. For example, it's good to keep the quilting evenly distributed across the quilt but if it works with the design not to, then don't. Since there aren't any rules involved, you can use design shortcuts when trying to decide your quilting design.

One of my favorite shortcuts is using the same quilting design in the same color across the entire quilt.

I did this on *Moving Through* (page 100). Each color has a different quilting design no matter where it is on the quilt.

Another shortcut is to quilt the background with one simple design and focus on adding details to the foreground space. This will eliminate the number of choices you have to make regarding your quilting

Close-up of the quilting on *Trellis* (page 64)

Photo by Heather Black

design. *Trellis* (page 64) is a good example of this; the background is quilted in straight lines but the blocks are more detailed.

Probably the most-used quilting design shortcut is to echo and repeat your design. This can mean echoing the quilt design itself or echoing other quilting. Repeating quilting designs is a good way to fill in spaces that are similar in size and shape. I did this on *Bird Watching* (page 54). I used the same quilting designs in the same shapes, repeating it for the entire quilt.

Quilting can be used to enhance a quilt design, but it can also work against a design. Pick quilting that will keep the depth in the design. In *Grounded* (page 93), all the quilting was chosen to enhance the depth of the design. I wanted to use the spiraling square in the center to draw the viewer's eye down and the quilting in the arms of the star are quilted in a way to make them look like they are extending upward. If I had used the background circles to quilt an allover design, some if not most of the depth in the design would have disappeared. If you have added depth to your quilt design, pick quilting that will keep or add to the depth.

Detail of *Bird Watching* (page 54)

Close-up of the quilting on *Grounded*.
See the project instructions (page 93).

You can also make layers with your quilting even if they aren't apparent in the quilt design. The best way to do this is to change the spacing in your quilting. Layers you want to appear closer to the viewer will be more widely spaced than layers that you want to appear further away. I use this technique when I want a background to recede into the distance. This is also a great way to maintain depth in your design.

Quilting can be used to add new quilt designs to your quilt, as well. On *Moving Through*'s lavender rectangles, I quilted a grid then filled it in with "messy" circles. By adding the grid, I was able to add a design element to the quilt and make the perfect backdrop for my circles.

In addition to adding a design element on *Moving Through*, I also created "ghost" shapes in the light blue and citron rectangles, flying geese and half-square triangles, respectively. Ghost shapes are a great way to fill in a large space and add interest to the quilt design. You can also use this technique to add text to your design. Remember that in general unquilted areas with show up more than quilted areas.

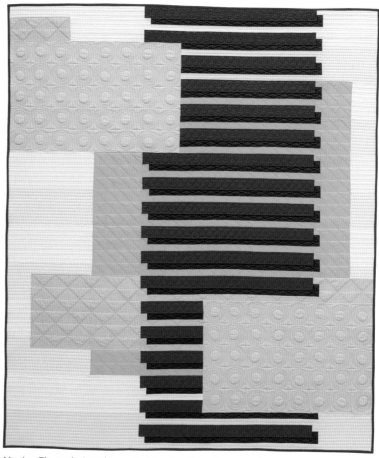

Moving Through. See the project instructions (page 100).

An exciting way to enhance your quilt is to add raw-edge appliqués in the quilting phase. It's a great way to create physical layers to your design, and at the same time add texture. This technique works best if you place the appliqués in an already quilted spot. On my *Make It Nine* (page 71) mini quilt, I first quilted the background in a wonky grid, then I added the circle appliqués by quilting them down, cutting them for more character, and adding more quilting. This is a great way to enhance a design, especially a design with limited piecing.

Detail of *Make it Nine* (page 71)

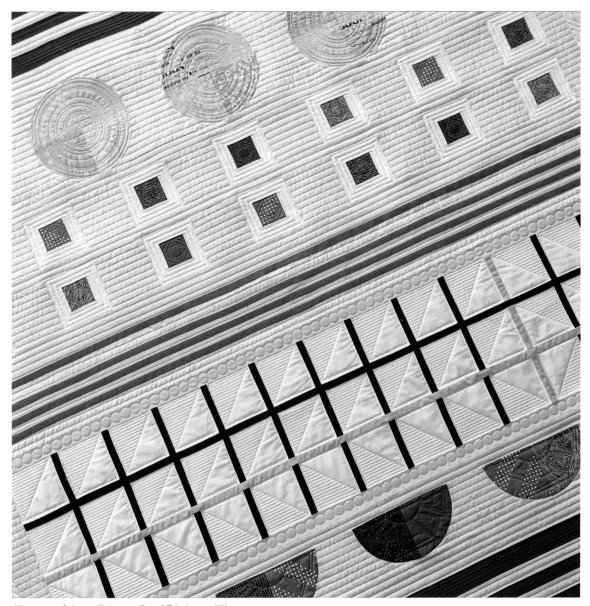

Close-up of the quilting on *Road Trip* (page 55)

Photo by Heather Black

Here are some quilting elements commonly found in modern quilting designs.

One of the most popular is to matchstick quilt an entire quilt design. I did this with *Around Town*. I want to create texture without taking away from the actual design elements in the quilt.

Close-up of *Around Town*, showing the matchstick quilting. See the project instructions (page 107)

Moving Through geometric quilting. See the project instructions (page 100)

Matchstick quilting is different to different people, but it is safe to call a straight, or nearly straight, line quilting less than ¼˝ apart matchstick. The secret to good matchstick quilting is to *not* space the lines equally. Equally spaced lines won't create the matchstick texture we all love, so make those lines crooked as long as they don't cross each other.

I added texture to the matchstick quilting by changing the thread colors. I used 9 thread colors on *Around Town* (page 107). Though not one color stands out over the others, it adds extra textures. To make the thread changes appear random, I changed out thread every first, third, fifth and seventh lines, a repeating pattern using odd numbers..

Geometric quilting designs are also found on many modern quilts. *Moving Through* (page 100) is covered in geometric quilting designs. The geese, half-square triangles, messy circles, straight lines, crisscross, and ribbon candy are all excellent examples of geometric quilting. Even though feathers and other free-form quilting designs can be found in modern quilting, they are less common than geometric and straight-line designs.

Close-up of *Trellis* (page 64), showing the mix of quilting

Detail of *Why Knot* (page 28)

Photo by Heather Black

I would also include graffiti quilting in this category. It mixes quilting design elements like swirls, pebbles, and grids seamlessly and is a great way to fill all the negative space that is so popular in modern quilts. *Trellis* (page 64) shows this mixing of textures and geometric shapes.

When quilting for a modern quilt design, just as with all the other design techniques, remember to keep the design true to your original quilt design and theme. Recall *Why Knot* (page 28)? The quilting on this design isn't particularly modern but it does follow my design theme—whimsy. The quilting in the background is still interlocking and looks like a knot, but the quilting in the arcs is more carefree and fun.

While the three modern quilting techniques are a great place to start or a good way to get past a difficult design decision, it's more important to have consistency in your design whether it is modern or not.

MAKING THE QUILT—
FROM DESIGN *to* REALITY

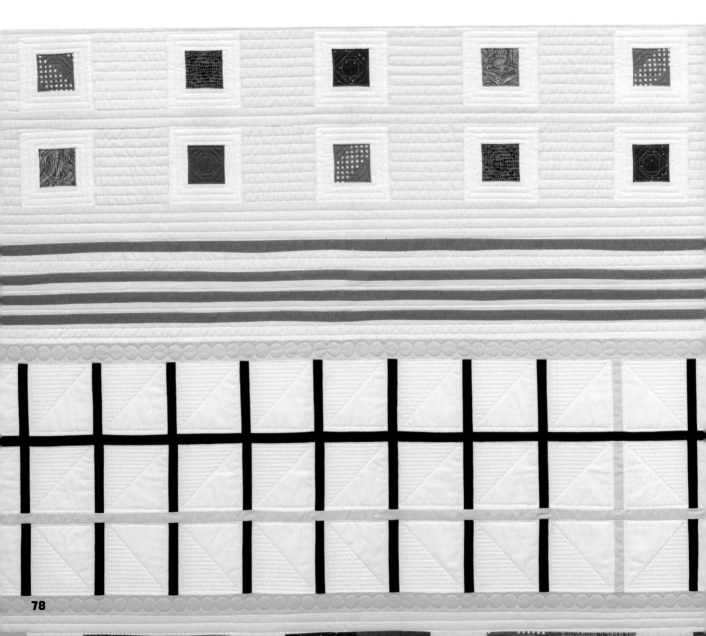

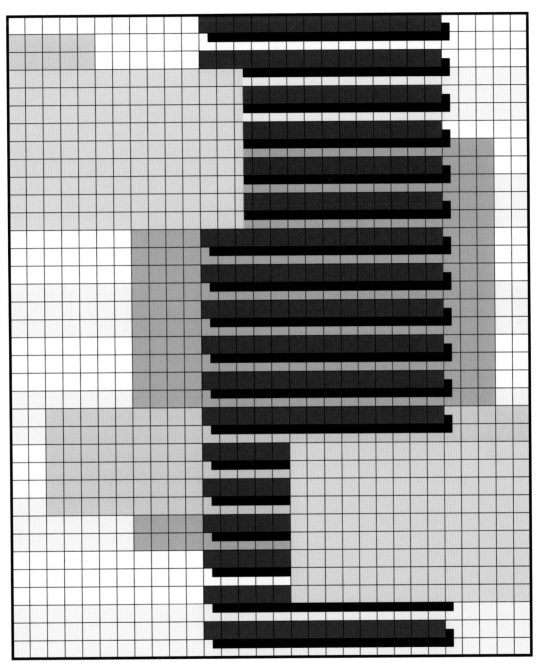

Moving Through (page 100) on a grid

Two items of quilt design that are frequently overlooked are backings and bindings. I try to think of backings as the hidden gem of the quilt. I love to find that one print that will work perfectly for my design, and since I make most of my quilts using solids, I tend to splurge on my backing fabric.

BACKINGS

When I'm looking for a backing, I don't focus as much on the color palette as I do on the theme of the quilt. I have run across plenty of prints that are the perfect color palette, but the theme of the print doesn't match the theme of the quilt. For example, I wouldn't buy a novelty print for an abstract quilt; okay, I may if the novelty print fits with the theme of the quilt.

You don't have to spend a day's salary to find the best quilt back for your design. A great way to make a corresponding quilt back is to piece it using fabrics from the quilt design. The important thing is to give that extra surprise to the viewer and pick a backing that won't distract from your quilt design. For *Stratagem* (page 35), I picked a backing that had the same feel as the theme of the quilt, a classic Parcheesi game board. Neither the quilt nor the backing was literally a Parcheesi game board, but they both convey the same feeling and fit in the theme.

The back of *Stratagem* (page 35)

Photo by Heather Black

BINDING

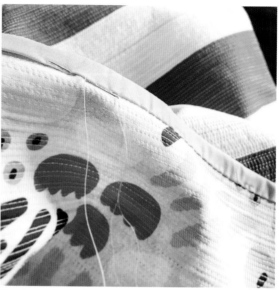

Photo by Heather Black

I consider the binding to be equivalent to the bow on a package or the eyeliner in your makeup routine. It can either make the whole design pop or it can distract. I have chosen bad bindings in my past and have even replaced a binding.

The easiest way to pick a binding is to pick a fabric from the design and make it the binding. This is what I did for all the quilts featured as projects in this book. I also try to pick a binding that completes the design.

In *Misprint* (page 119), I matched the binding to the piecing on the edge of the quilt design. Binding can be a continuation of a design element. In *Stratagem* (page 35), I used the binding to make one side of the frame around the blocks.

A binding can also steer the quilt design in a new direction. On *Bird Watching* (page 54), I used a print with the same color palette to soften the bold geometric design.

Bindings can also complement a design. For *Road Trip* (page 55), I picked a dusty lavender that complemented the color palette even though it was not in the original quilt design. Don't neglect those bindings; they can really make a statement.

The bindings shine in this stack of quilts.

Photo by Heather Black

It is also an option not to have a binding at all. I've never had a design that I didn't want to add a binding to, even my mini quilts, but sometimes a binding adds nothing to the design or even takes away from the overall look of the quilt. In those situations, I recommend facing your quilt. Facing is a way of finishing your quilt without having any visible binding on the front of the quilt. This is a great option for smaller quilts, quilts without borders, and even art quilts.

It will make a big difference in your finished quilt if you take a bit of time to think through your choice in terms of your quilt design and theme. If you still don't think backing and bindings make a difference, consider this: I frequently receive praise for my backing choice and bindings in the judge's notes from quilt shows.

BONUS FEATURES OF A GRID

Using a grid in all your quilt designs will give your designs balance, but it will also make it easier to determine your piecing and fabric needs for the design. There's no guesswork; you can use the grid to know the exact size of each unit in the quilt. I've even taken a picture of a quilt design and been able to piece it on the spot without any reference to unit sizes because I knew what size grid I used to design it. A grid is also a good way to catch mistakes before cutting into any fabric. If you know you've designed a quilt on a 6″ grid but you made a note to cut 5″ squares, it's easy to catch that error before it becomes a costly mistake.

Once you know the size of the units you need for your design, you can calculate fabric yardage. Calculating yardage can be intimidating, but it really is just a simple method. The best way to calculate yardage is to figure out how many of one type of unit will fit in the width of fabric.

For my patterns, I assume the width of fabric to be 40″. For example, if you need 50 squares 6″ × 6″ and want to calculate the yardage for that, first add ½″ to the width and depth measurements to account for the seam allowance; then divide the width of fabric (in this case 40″) by the length of the square (6½″): 40 ÷ 6½ = 6.15 units. Next round *down* to the nearest whole number (6), then divide that into the number of squares needed: 50 ÷ 6 = 8.33. This time round *up* to the nearest whole number (9); this gives you the number of width-of-fabric strips needed to cut 50 squares 6½″ × 6½″.

To determine how much total fabric you need, multiply the number of strips needed (9) by the width of the unfinished square (6½″): 9″ × 6½″ = 58.5″.

At this point, you have two choices. You can add an additional width-of-fabric strip for the widest width needed for the design (in this case 6½″) for a total of 65″ of fabric (1⅞ yards): 65″ ÷ 36″ = 1.80 yards. Or you can add 10% more fabric (58.5″ × 10% = 5.85″) for a total of 64.35″: 64.35″ ÷ 36″ = 1.79 yards. In this case, both options will require 1⅞ yards of fabric; but depending on the size of units, I will use one technique over the other. In this example, I would use the first technique of adding another 6½″ width-of-fabric strip. If in addition to the 50 squares 6½″ × 6½″ I needed 1 square 10½″ × 10½″, I would use the second technique because there is no reason to add another 10½″ width-of-fabric strip when you can cut more than one on the same width-of-fabric strip.

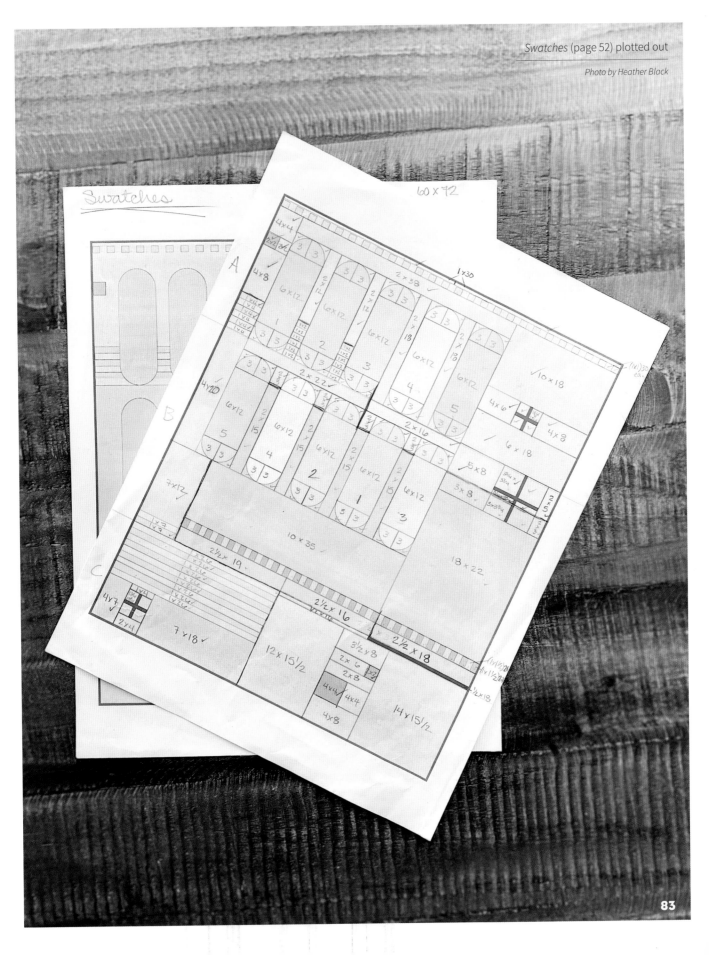

Calculating yardage

Photo by Heather Black

TIP

Don't forget to add ½″ to all finished block and piece measurements to account for the seam allowance.

Using a grid is great for design but it is also great for getting that design to a place where you can make it a quilt. So, take advantage of all the benefits of using a grid.

SELECTING FABRICS

Pulling fabric

Photo by Heather Black

Your first and best guide to choosing fabrics is your design theme. Matching fabrics to the colors in the design is the fastest way to pull fabrics. If you are looking for an exact match for your design, it's best to go with solid fabrics. Many fabric companies have a line of solids that often coordinate with the colors in the prints they make. The projects in this book use Painter's Palette Solids by Paintbrush Studio Fabrics. When picking solids, it's important to remember that you're not just looking for the right color or hue, but you may also need to match a shade/tint of that hue, saturation, or value.

Painter's Palette Solids
by Paintbrush Studio Fabrics

Photo by Heather Black

Near-solid fabrics

Photo by Heather Black

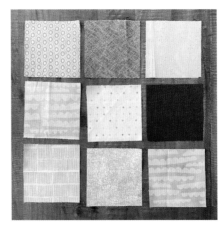

Prints that read as solid

Photo by Heather Black

The next fabric choice for closely matching your quilt design is to choose prints that are nearly solids or read as solids. A near-solid fabric is one that has an overwhelming color, usually in the background, and a limited amount of foreground printing. Texture prints and dyed fabrics are great examples of near solids.

Prints that read as solid may have a large number of different colors in the print, but at a distance they will visually read as a single color. There are prints that read as solids that are only two or three colors, too. Many of those will have colors that are similar in appearance, such as a yellow background and cream foreground that at a distance appear to be only yellow.

Small prints

Photo by Heather Black

Medium prints

Photo by Heather Black

Near-solid and prints that read as solid are good way to introduce some interest in a design without disturbing the overall color palette.

Small-to-medium-sized prints are a great way to add layers and movement to your design. They can subtly change colors and add interest to a design. When I designed *Road Trip* (page 55) I used a very mild color palette. But when I went to make the quilt, I knew I wanted to have the feeling of motion, since it is representing looking out a car window. I added prints to the yellow circles, green squares, and green half-circles. These prints were a mix of read-as-solids and medium-sized prints. In some, you can barely see that they are prints, but others have a clear color change or design. These add interest, depth, and movement to the quilt. Small to medium prints are a great way to experiment with prints and see how they change your design. Most quilts are made with combinations of medium-sized prints.

Close-up of *Road Trip* (page 55)

Large-scale prints

Photo by Heather Black

Large-scale prints have elements that are typically distorted or unrecognizable if cut into smaller pieces. I love these prints for backing, but they can be hard to incorporate into a quilt design with smaller units. These prints can be a fabulous way to introduce a surprise element in the design, a peek-a-boo moment. In *The Cool Kids* (page 60), I used a large-scale print as a way of showing what was behind the black circle. Large-scale prints can add an extra layer to your quilt design and cutting them up is a good way to create mystique.

Close-up of *The Cool Kids* (page 60)

Detail of *Stratagem* (page 35)

There can be several ways to execute your quilt design: traditional piecing, paper piecing, improv piecing, appliqué, or a mixture of techniques. How you piece your quilt will affect the design in different ways and some piecing techniques may not work with your design at all. If you've designed a quilt that is very ridged and structured, and you want to keep that theme, don't choose free-flowing improv piecing. A technique like paper piecing will probably be a better fit. Staying true to your design and theme will be the best option when trying to decide how to execute your design.

Choosing a piecing technique can be practical as well as creative. Some designs can be executed only one certain way. Some shapes need to be appliquéd; others need to be improv pieced. The necessity of a piecing technique will drive your choice, but if you know you don't like to appliqué, don't design a quilt that requires appliqué.

Pressing can affect your design as well. If you have to press your seams open, no questions asked; or if pressing to the dark side is all muscle memory, you may not care what pressing can do for a design. But if you are open to different pressing techniques while piecing your quilt, there are a few details to consider.

Detail of raw-edge appliqué in *Make It Nine* (page 71)

Sometimes pressing to one side can make one piecing unit look like it is sitting on top of the other. This can be problematic if the pressing is fighting what you're are trying to do with the design.

Likewise, pressing seams open will flatten your piecing. If the design depth in the design can't withstand a flattening, you may want to press the seam to one side.

I personally press all my seams open, even my curve piecing, but if I had a low-volume quilt or a monotone quilt, I would consider pressing to one side to further my design goals. In a lower-contrast design, it can be harder to convey depth. Using pressing to make one design element lay on top of the other can make a difference. For example, when you press a curve toward the convex unit, it will appear as if the quarter-circle is sitting on top of the background. But if you press the curve to the concave unit, it will look as if the quarter-circle is under the background fabric.

Photo by Heather Black

PROJECTS

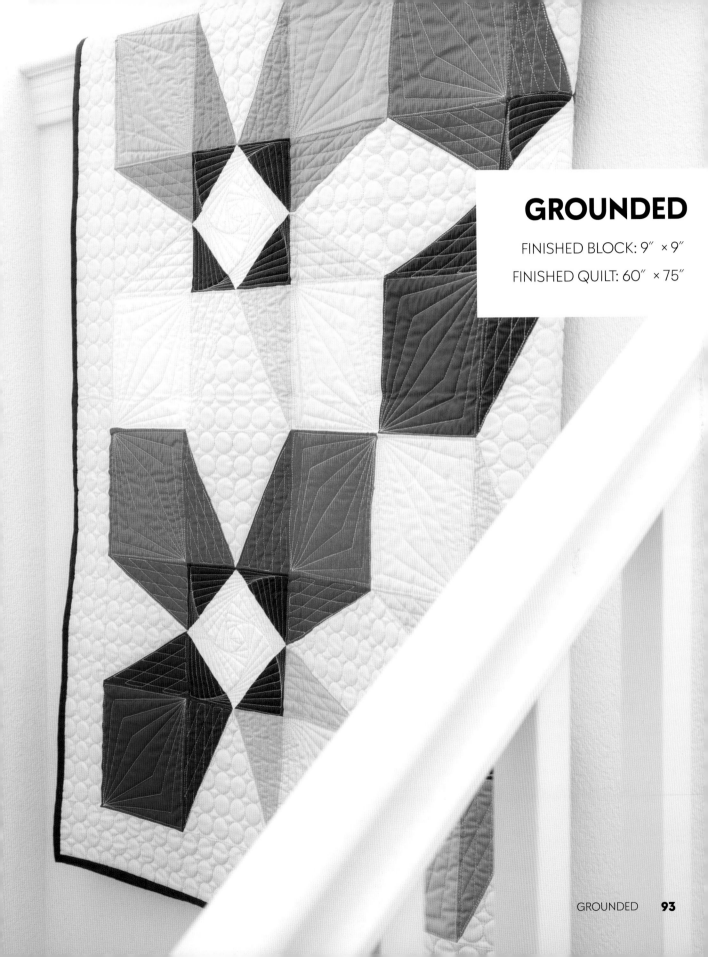

GROUNDED

FINISHED BLOCK: 9″ × 9″

FINISHED QUILT: 60″ × 75″

Need a huge impact without all the work? *Grounded* uses color to create depth and transparency. Add more interest by selecting an unexpected color palette and a nontraditional background color. The offset border and navy-and-white centers ground the colors and the design.

MATERIALS

Yardages are based on 40˝ usable width.

Background

AQUA (Limelight*): 1⅞ yards

Half-square triangles

NAVY (Navy*): ½ yard

WHITE (Rice Paper*): ½ yard

Half-rectangles

Pair A: Off-white

LIGHT (Oyster*): ⅜ yard

DARK (Linen*): ⅜ yard

Pair B: Blue-gray

LIGHT (Sky*): ⅜ yard

DARK (Cracked Ice*): ⅜ yard

Pair C: Blue

LIGHT (River Blue*): ⅜ yard

DARK (French Blue*): ⅜ yard

Pair D: Red

LIGHT (Tomato*): ⅜ yard

DARK (Christmas Red*): ⅜ yard

Pair E: Magenta

LIGHT (Rosebud*): ⅜ yard

DARK (Sangria*): ⅜ yard

Pair F: Yellow

LIGHT (Maize*): ⅜ yard

DARK (Sulfur*): ⅜ yard

Pair G: Green

LIGHT (Frolic*): ⅜ yard

DARK (Wasabi*): ⅜ yard

Pair H: Orange

LIGHT (Golden Rod*): ⅜ yard

DARK (Bronze*): ⅜ yard

Pair I: Gray

LIGHT (Mist*): ⅜ yard

DARK (Ash*): ⅜ yard

Pair J: Pink

LIGHT (Rose*): ⅜ yard

DARK (Petunia*): ⅜ yard

Additional

BINDING: ⅝ yard

BACKING: 4¾ yards

BATTING: Twin size (I recommend Hobbs Tuscany Cotton/Wool Batting.)

> **Fabrics I used:**
> * *Painter's Palette Solids by Paintbrush Studio Fabrics*

CUTTING

Make a template from the 6˝ Half-Rectangle Triangle pattern (page 99).

Aqua

- Cut 6 strips 6½˝ × width of fabric.

  Subcut 96 half-rectangles, 48 right-facing and 48 left-facing, using the half-rectangle triangle template and referring to the half-rectangle triangle cutting diagram.

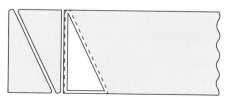

Half-rectangle triangle cutting

Fold the width-of-fabric strip in half. Use the template to cut half-rectangle triangles, 2 at a time from the folded strip, to yield 1 right-facing and 1 left-facing half-rectangle triangle with each cut.

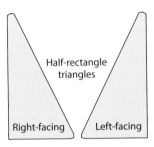

Half-rectangle triangles

Right-facing | Left-facing

• Cut 6 strips 3½˝ × width of fabric. Subcut:

 4 rectangles 3½˝ × 36½˝ for side borders

 2 rectangles 3½˝ × 30½˝ for bottom border

Navy

• Cut 2 strips 6˝ × width of fabric. Subcut 12 squares 6˝ × 6˝.

White

• Cut 2 strips 6˝ × width of fabric. Subcut 12 squares 6˝ × 6˝.

Pairs A–H

• **From each light fabric:** Cut 5 squares 6½˝ × 6½˝.

• **From each dark fabric:** Cut 1 strip 6½˝ × width of fabric.

 Subcut 10 half-rectangle triangles, 5 right-facing and 5 left-facing, using the half-rectangle triangle template.

Pairs I and J

• **From each light fabric:** Cut 4 squares 6½˝ × 6½˝.

• **From each dark fabric:** Cut 1 strip 6½˝ × width of fabric.

 Subcut 8 half-rectangle triangles, 4 right-facing and 4 left-facing, using the half-rectangle triangle template.

Binding

• Cut 8 strips 2½˝ × width of fabric.

CONSTRUCTION

Half-Square Triangles

Use the following method to create 48 navy/white half-square triangle units.

1. Place a navy 6˝ × 6˝ square and a white 6˝ × 6˝ square right sides together.

2. Sew ¼˝ from the outside edge all around the layered navy and white squares.

3. Cut the layered squares in half diagonally in both directions, creating 4 half-square triangles. Be careful not to move the pieces as you cut.

Cut from corner to corner.

4. Press open the 4 navy/white half-square triangle units, begin careful not to stretch the bias edges.

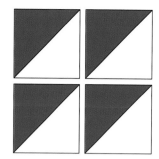

5. Trim and square each of the half-square triangle units to 3½″ × 3½″.

6. Repeat Steps 1–5 to make a total of 48 navy/white half-square triangle units.

Half-Rectangle Triangles

Each half-rectangle triangle unit is made with 1 aqua half-rectangle and 1 dark half-rectangle.

1. Sew 1 left-facing aqua half-rectangle triangle to a pair A dark left-facing half-rectangle triangle.

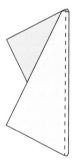

2. Press open, creating a left-facing half-rectangle triangle unit.

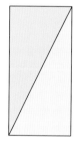

3. Sew 1 right-facing aqua half-rectangle triangle to a pair A dark right-facing half-rectangle triangle.

4. Press open, creating a right-facing half-rectangle triangle unit.

5. Repeat Steps 1–4 for the remaining dark left- and right-facing half-rectangle triangles from pair A for a total of 5 mirror-image half-rectangle triangle unit pairs.

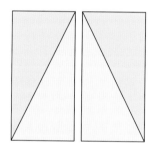

6. Repeat Steps 1–5 for the remaining dark half-rectangle triangles for pairs B–J. Please note that the dark fabric for pairs I and J will yield only 4 mirror-image half-rectangle triangle units.

Block Assembly

Refer to the block assembly diagram (below).

1. Sew a 6½˝ × 6½˝ square to a left-facing half-rectangle triangle unit from pair A.

2. Sew a navy/white half-square triangle to a right-facing half-rectangle triangle unit.

3. Sew the units together to complete the block.

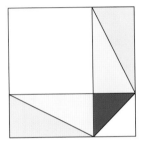

Block assembly

TIP

The square is always matched to the "dark" side of the half-rectangle triangle unit.

4. Repeat Steps 1–3 to make a total of 5 pair A blocks.

5. Repeat Steps 1–4 for pairs A–J, keeping in mind that there will be only 4 blocks for pairs I and J.

Borders

1. Make each of the 2 side borders by sewing 2 rectangles 3½˝ × 36½˝ end to end to create a strip 3½˝ × 72½˝.

2. Make the bottom border by sewing 2 rectangles 3½˝ × 30½˝ end to end to create a strip 3½˝ × 60½˝.

QUILT ASSEMBLY

1. Following the quilt assembly diagram, sew the blocks into rows, and then sew the rows together for the quilt body.

2. Sew the right border to the quilt body.

3. Sew the left border to the quilt body.

4. Sew the bottom border to the quilt body to complete the quilt top.

Quilt assembly

Finishing

1. Divide the backing into 2 lengths. Sew the panels together lengthwise. The seam will be vertical down the back of the quilt.

2. Layer, quilt, and bind as desired.

Grounded, 60˝ × 75˝, designed, pieced, and quilted by Heather Black

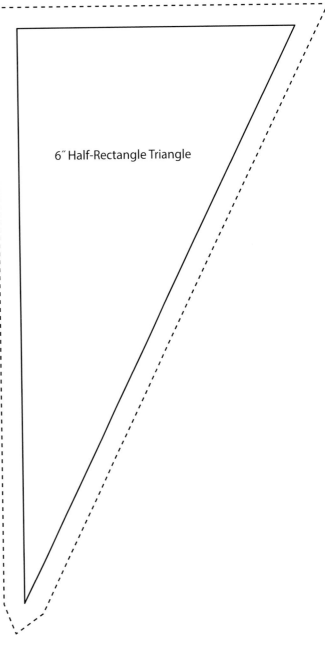

6″ Half-Rectangle Triangle

MOVING THROUGH

FINISHED BLOCK: BASED ON A 2″ GRID

FINISHED QUILT: 60″ × 72″

A quilt design with this many lines can't help but have movement. *Moving Through* is a great quilt for using color, shadows, and lines to create layers and depth along with movement. This quilt is perfect for trying out modern quilting motifs in large color blocked areas.

MATERIALS

Yardages are based on 40˝ usable width.

ROYAL BLUE (French Blue*): 1⅝ yards, binding included

LAVENDER (Sachet*): 1⅓ yards

CHARTREUSE (Lemon Ice*): 1 yard

WHITE (Rice Paper*): 1 yard

PINK (Pale Pink*): 1 yard

CHARCOAL (Smoke*): ¾ yard

PALE BLUE (Cracked Ice*): ⅔ yard

BACKING (Bloom**): 3⅞ yards

BATTING: Twin size (I recommend Hobbs Tuscany Cotton/Wool Batting.)

> **Fabrics I used:** * Painter's Palette Solids by Paintbrush Studio Fabrics
> ** Print Bloom 120-20101 by Paintbrush Studio Fabrics

CUTTING

Royal blue

- Cut 21 strips 2½˝ × width of fabric. Subcut:

  9 rectangles 2½˝ × 28½˝

  4 rectangles 2½˝ × 22½˝

  5 rectangles 2½˝ × 10½˝

  Set aside remaining strips 2½˝ × width of fabric for binding.

Lavender

- Cut 2 strips 18½˝ × width of fabric. Subcut:

  1 rectangle 18½˝ × 22½˝

  1 rectangle 18½˝ × 19½˝

  1 rectangle 18½˝ × 9½˝

  1 rectangle 18½˝ × 6½˝

Chartreuse

- Cut 1 strip 8½˝ × width of fabric. Subcut:

  1 rectangle 8½˝ × 20½˝

  1 rectangle 8½˝ × 4½˝

- Cut 1 strip 5½˝ × width of fabric. Subcut 1 rectangle 5½˝ × 32½˝.

- Cut 8 strips 1½˝ × width of fabric. Subcut:

  5 rectangles 1½˝ × 29½˝

  3 rectangles 1½˝ × 23½˝

  1 rectangle 1½˝ × 10½˝

  14 squares 1½˝ × 1½˝

White

- Cut 3 strips 6½˝ × width of fabric. Subcut:

  1 rectangle 6½˝ × 22½˝

  2 rectangles 6½˝ × 14½˝

  1 rectangle 6½˝ × 12½˝

  1 rectangle 6½˝ × 9½˝

  4 rectangles 6½˝ × 4½˝

  1 rectangle 2½˝ × 10½˝

- Cut 2 strips 1½˝ × width of fabric. Subcut:

  1 rectangle 1½˝ × 29½˝

  1 rectangle 1½˝ × 10½˝

  4 squares 1½˝ × 1½˝

Pink

- Cut 3 strips 6½″ × width of fabric. Subcut:

  1 rectangle 6½″ × 22½″

  1 rectangle 6½″ × 14½″

  2 rectangles 6½″ × 9½″

  4 rectangles 4½″ × ½″

  1 rectangle 4½″ × 10½″

- Cut 1 strip 2½″ × width of fabric. Subcut:

  1 rectangle 2½″ × 10½″

  1 rectangle 2½″ × 4½″

- Cut 4 strips 1½″ × width of fabric. Subcut:

  2 rectangles 1½″ × 29½″

  2 rectangles 1½″ × 23½″

  4 squares 1½″ × 1½″

Charcoal

- Cut 14 strips 1½″ × width of fabric. Subcut:

  9 rectangles 1½″ × 28½″

  5 rectangles 1½″ × 23½″

  4 rectangles 1½″ × 9½″

  13 squares 1½″ × 1½″

Pale blue

- Cut 1 strip 10½″ × width of fabric. Subcut:

  1 rectangle 10½″ × 12½″

  1 rectangle 10½″ × 4½″

  1 rectangle 9½″ × 4½″

  1 rectangle 8½″ × 12½″

- Cut 2 strips 1½″ × width of fabric. Subcut:

  1 rectangle 1½″ × 29½″

  2 rectangles 1½″ × 10½″

  4 squares 1½″ × 1½″

CONSTRUCTION

Column A

Refer to the Column A assembly diagram (next page).

Section A1

1. Sew a white 10½″ × 2½″ rectangle to the top of a pale blue 10½″ × 2½″ rectangle lengthwise.

2. Sew a white 12½″ × 6½″ rectangle to the right side of the unit from Step 1.

Section A3

1. Sew a white 14½″ × 6½″ rectangle to the top and bottom of a pink 14½″ × 6½″ rectangle.

2. Sew a pink 10½″ × 2½″ rectangle to the top of a pale blue 10½″ × 12½″ rectangle. Sew a pink 10½″ × 4½″ rectangle to the bottom of the unit.

3. Sew a pink 4½″ × 6½″ rectangle to the top and bottom of a white 4½″ × 6½″ rectangle.

4. Sew the unit from Step 3 to the left side of the unit from Step 2.

5. Sew the unit from Step 1 to the top of the unit from Step 4.

Section A4

Sew a chartreuse 8½″ × 20½″ rectangle to the top of a pale blue 8½″ × 12½″ rectangle. Sew a chartreuse 8½″ × 4½″ rectangle to the bottom of the unit.

Section A5

Sew a white 22½″ × 6½″ rectangle to the top of a pink 22½″ × 6½″ rectangle.

Column A Assembly

1. Sew section A3 to the left side of section A4, remembering to match up the pale blue rectangles.

2. Sew sections A1, A2 (lavender 22½″ × 18½″ rectangle), A3/A4, and A5 together to complete the column.

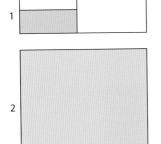

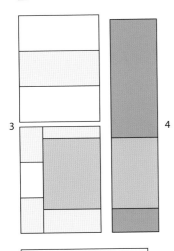

Column A assembly

Column B

Refer to the Column B assembly diagram (page 104).

Section B1

1. Sew a white 1½″ × 1½″ square to a charcoal 1½″ × 1½″ square. Make 2.

2. Sew a unit from Step 1 to the right end of a royal blue 28½″ × 2½″ rectangle. Make 2.

3. Sew a white 1½″ × 1½″ square to the left end of a charcoal 28½″ × 1½″ rectangle.

4. Following the diagram, sew the above units and a white 29½″ × 1½″ rectangle together.

Section B2

1. Sew a pink 1½″ × 1½″ square to a charcoal 1½″ × 1½″ square.

2. Sew a chartreuse 1½″ × 1½″ square to 1 charcoal 1½″ × 1½″ square. Make 3.

3. Sew a unit from Step 1 to the right end of a royal blue 22½″ × 2½″ rectangle.

4. Sew a unit from Step 2 to the right end of a royal blue 22½″ × 2½″ rectangle. Make 3.

5. Following the diagram, sew the above units together with 2 pink 23½″ × 1½″ rectangles, 3 chartreuse 23½″ × 1½″ rectangles, 5 charcoal 23½″ × 1½″ rectangles, and 1 lavender 6½″ × 18½″ rectangle.

Section B3

1. Sew a pale blue 1½″ × 1½″ square to a charcoal 1½″ × 1½″ square.

2. Sew the unit from Step 1 to the right end of a royal blue 28½″ × 2½″ rectangle.

3. Sew a chartreuse 1½˝ × 1½˝ square to 1 charcoal 1½˝ × 1½˝ square. Make 5.

4. Sew a unit from Step 3 to the right end of a royal blue 28½˝ × 2½˝ rectangle. Make 5.

5. Sew a pale blue 1½˝ × 1½˝ square to the left end of a charcoal 28½˝ × 1½˝ rectangle.

6. Sew a chartreuse 1½˝ × 1½˝ square to the left end of a charcoal 28½˝ × 1½˝ rectangle. Make 5.

7. Following the diagram, sew the above units together with a pale blue 29½˝ × 1½˝ rectangle, and 5 chartreuse 29½˝ × 1½˝ rectangles.

Section B4

1. Sew a pale blue 1½˝ × 1½˝ square to the left end of a charcoal 9½˝ × 1½˝ rectangle. Make 2.

2. Sew a chartreuse 1½˝ × 1½˝ square to the left end of a charcoal 9½˝ × 1½˝ rectangle.

3. Sew a white 1½˝ × 1½˝ square to the left end of a charcoal 9½˝ × 1½˝ rectangle.

4. Following the diagram, sew the above units together with 2 pale blue 10½˝ × 1½˝ rectangles, a chartreuse 10½˝ × 1½˝ rectangle, a white 10½˝ × 1½˝ rectangle, and 5 royal blue 10½˝ × 2½˝ rectangles.

5. Sew a lavender 19½˝ × 18½˝ rectangle to the right side of the unit from Step 4.

Section B5

1. Sew a pink 1½˝ × 1½˝ square to the left end of charcoal 28½˝ × 1½˝ rectangle. Make 2.

2. Sew a pink 1½˝ × 1½˝ square to a charcoal 1½˝ × 1½˝ square.

3. Sew the unit from Step 2 to the right end of a royal blue 28½˝ × 2½˝ rectangle.

4. Following the diagram, sew the above units together with 2 pink 29½˝ × 1½˝ rectangles.

Column B Assembly

Sew sections B1, B2, B3, B4, and B5 together.

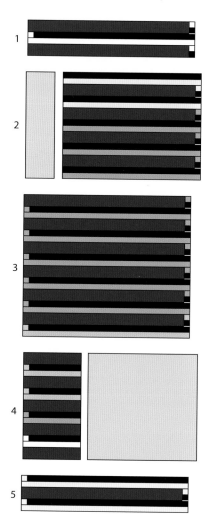

Column B assembly

Column C

Refer to the Column C assembly diagram (below).

Section C1

Sew a white 9½″ × 6½″ rectangle to the top of a pink 9½″ × 6½″ rectangle.

Section C2

1. Sew 3 white 4½″ × 6½″ rectangles and 2 pink 4½″ × 6½″ rectangles end to end, alternating colors.

2. Sew a pink 4½″ × 2½″ rectangle to the bottom of the pink/white unit.

3. Sew a chartreuse 5½″ × 32½″ rectangle to the left side of the pink/white unit.

Section C3

1. Sew a pale blue 9½″ × 4½″ rectangle to the top of a lavender 9½″ × 18½″ rectangle C.

2. Sew a pink 9½″ × 6½″ rectangle to the bottom of the lavender/pale blue unit.

Column C Assembly

Sew sections C1, C2, and C3 together end to end.

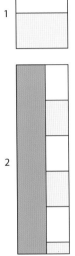

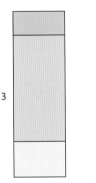

Column C assembly

QUILT ASSEMBLY

Following the quilt assembly diagram, sew columns A, B, and C side by side to complete the quilt top.

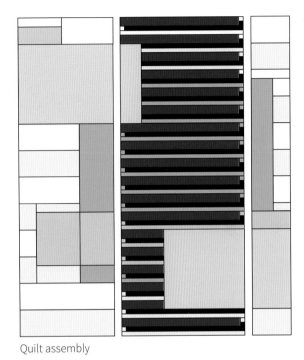

Quilt assembly

Finishing

1. Divide the backing into 2 lengths. Sew the panels crosswise. The seam will be horizontal across the back of the quilt.

2. Layer, quilt, and bind as desired.

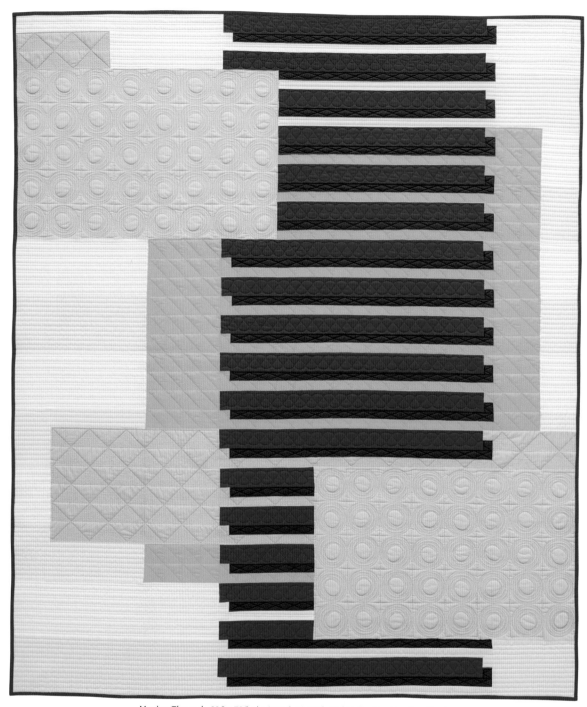

Moving Through, 60″ × 72″, designed, pieced, and quilted by Heather Black

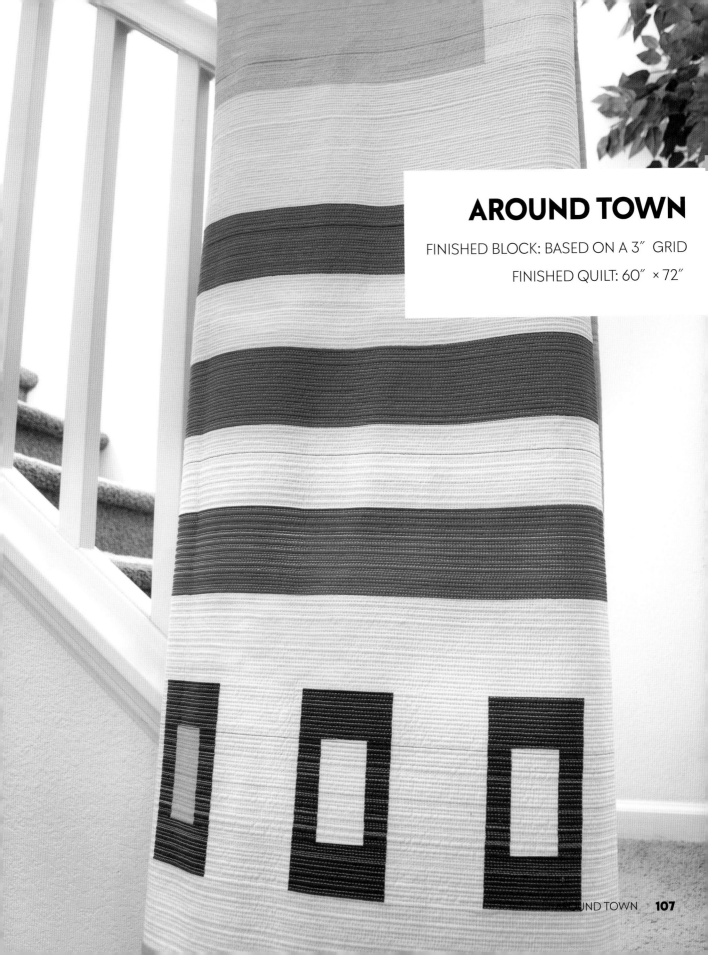

AROUND TOWN

FINISHED BLOCK: BASED ON A 3″ GRID

FINISHED QUILT: 60″ × 72″

Around Town focuses on captured sights and shapes from a drive around town—hints of windows and buildings, bridges and arches. This design focuses on maintaining balance with a hidden 3″ grid. The color palette adds depth and movement.

MATERIALS

Yardages are based on 40″ usable width.

CHARTREUSE (Lemon Ice*): 1⅓ yards, binding included

CREAM (Snow*): 1⅓ yards

PINK (Pale Pink*): 1⅓ yards

CHARCOAL (Smoke*): ¾ yard

AQUA (Limelight*): ¾ yard

RED (Fireworks*): ⅝ yard

TURQUOISE (Turquoise*): ½ yard

WHITE (Rice Paper*): ⅓ yard

NAVY (Cadet*): ⅛ yard

BACKING (Large Floral Pink**): 3⅞ yards for backing

BATTING: Twin size (I recommend Hobbs Tuscany Cotton/Wool Batting.)

Fabrics I used:	* *Painter's Palette Solids by Paintbrush Studio Fabrics* ** *Garden Glory by Paintbrush Studio Fabrics*

CUTTING

Make templates from these patterns: 6″ Concave (page 118), 6″ Arc (page 118), 6″ Convex (page 117), and 3″ Convex (page 117). Cut the convex, concave, and arc units using the templates.

Chartreuse

- Cut 1 strip 6½″ × width of fabric. Subcut 1 rectangle 6½″ × 27½″.

- Cut 4 strips 3½″ × width of fabric. Subcut:

  3 rectangles 3½″ × 27½″

  3 rectangles 3½″ × 9½″

  9 squares 3½″ × 3½″

- Cut 8 strips 2½″ × width of fabric for binding.

Cream

- Cut 3 strips 6½″ × width of fabric. Subcut:

  1 rectangle 6½″ × 15½″

  1 square 6½″ × 6½″

  11 rectangles 6½″ × 3½″

  6 concave pieces, using the 6″ template

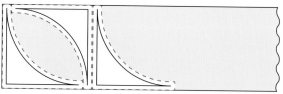

Concave cutting

- Cut 5 strips 3½″ × width of fabric. Subcut:

  4 rectangles 3½″ × 21½″

  3 rectangles 3½″ × 18½″

  1 rectangle 3½″ × 15½″

  2 rectangles 3½″ × 9½″

  3 squares 3½″ × 3½″

Pink

- Cut 2 strips 6½″ × width of fabric. Subcut:

  1 rectangle 6½″ × 27½″

  2 rectangles 6½″ × 18½″

  2 concave pieces, using the 6″ template

- Cut 8 strips 3½″ × width of fabric. Subcut:

  2 rectangles 3½″ × 27½″

  6 rectangles 3½″ × 24½″

  2 rectangles 3½″ × 6½″

  15 squares 3½″ × 3½″

Charcoal

- Cut 2 strips 6½″ × width of fabric. Subcut:

  9 rectangles 6½″ × 3½″

  3 rectangles 6½″ × 2½″

  3 rectangles 6½″ × 2″

- Cut 2 strips 3½″ × width of fabric. Subcut:

  14 rectangles 3½″ × 2″

  14 rectangles 3½″ × 1¼″

Aqua

- Cut 1 strip 6½″ × width of fabric. Subcut:

  1 rectangle 6½″ × 12½″

  4 concave pieces, using the 6″ template

  1 rectangle 6½″ × 3½″

- Cut 4 strips 3½″ × width of fabric. Subcut:

  3 rectangles 3½″ × 27½″

  1 rectangles 3½″ × 15½″

  3 rectangles 3½″ × 12½″

  3 squares 3½″ × 3½″

Red

- Cut 2 strips 6½″ × width of fabric. Subcut:

  8 convex pieces, using the 6″ template

  4 arc pieces, using the 6″ template

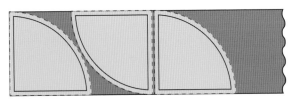

Convex cutting

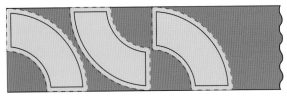

Arc cutting

Turquoise

- Cut 3 strips 3½″ × width of fabric. Subcut:

  3 rectangles 3½″ × 36½″

  2 convex pieces, using the 3″ template

- Cut 1 strip 1½″ × width of fabric. Subcut
  3 rectangles 1½″ × 6½″.

White

- Cut 2 strips 3½″ × width of fabric. Subcut:

  9 squares 3½″ × 3½″

  5 rectangles 2″ × 3½″

  2 convex pieces, using the 3″ template

Navy

- Cut 1 strip 2″ × width of fabric. Subcut 3 rectangles
  2″ × 6½″.

CONSTRUCTION

Half-Circle Blocks

Sew a red convex unit to an aqua concave unit, right sides together, by following these steps.

1. Mark the center of the convex piece by folding it in half along the curve and finger-pressing a crease. Do the same for the concave piece.

2. Place the concave piece on top of the convex piece, right sides together.

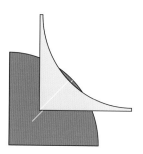

3. Line up the center creases and pin.

4. Finish by pinning along the curve as needed.

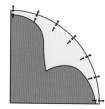

5. Sew along the curve with a scant ¼˝ seam allowance, removing the pins as you sew.

6. Press the seam open, creating a quarter-circle unit.

7. Repeat Steps 1–6 to make a total of 4 aqua/red quarter-circles and 4 cream/red quarter-circles.

8. Sew 2 matching quarter-circle units together to make a half-circle block.

9. Repeat Step 8 for a total of 2 aqua/red half-circles and 2 cream/red half-circles.

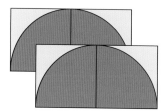

Make 2.

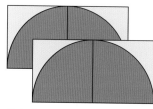

Make 2.

Double Half-Circle Blocks

Sew a turquoise convex piece, a red arc, and a cream concave piece right sides together following these steps:

1. Fold and crease at the center of 1 turquoise convex piece and 1 red arc.

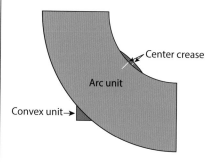

2. Place a red arc on top of a turquoise convex piece. Line up the curves at the center and pin in place as needed, see diagram.

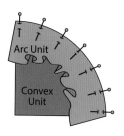

3. Sew a turquoise convex and a red arc together using a scant ¼˝ seam. Press open to create a large convex unit.

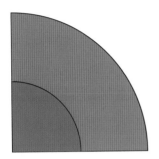

4. Fold and crease at the center of the large convex unit and 1 cream concave piece.

5. Place the cream concave unit on top of 1 large convex unit. Line up the curves at the center and pin in place as needed.

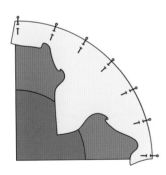

6. Sew the large convex and cream concave units together using a scant ¼˝ seam. Press open to create a cream / red / turquoise quarter-circle block.

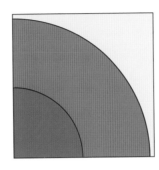

7. Repeat Steps 1–6 to make a total of 2 cream / red / turquoise quarter-circle blocks and 2 pink / red / white quarter-circle blocks.

8. Sew matching quarter-circle blocks to make a cream / red / turquoise half-circle block and a pink / red / white half-circle block.

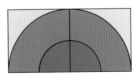

Make 1.

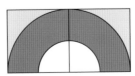

Make 1.

Door Blocks

1. Sew a charcoal 2½˝ × 6½˝ rectangle to the left side of a turquoise 1½˝ × 6½˝ rectangle. Make 3.

Make 3.

2. Sew a charcoal 2˝ × 6½˝ rectangle to the left side of a navy 2˝ × 6½˝ rectangle. Make 3.

Make 3.

3. Set aside the 9 charcoal 3½˝ × 6½˝ rectangles to serve as the remaining door blocks when you assemble section B.

Window Blocks

1. Sew a charcoal 1¼″ × 3½″ rectangle to the left and right sides of a white 2″ × 3½″ rectangle. Sew a charcoal 3½″ × 2″ rectangle to the top and bottom of the white/charcoal unit. Make 5.

Make 5.

2. Sew a charcoal 1¼″ × 3½″ rectangle to the left and right sides of a chartreuse 2″ × 3½″ rectangle. Sew a charcoal 3½″ × 2″ rectangle to the top and bottom of the chartreuse/charcoal unit. Make 2.

Make 2.

Section A

Please refer to the Section A assembly diagram (below).

1. Sew an aqua 12½″ × 3½″ rectangle to the top and bottom of an aqua 12½″ × 6½″ rectangle, creating an aqua 12½″ × 12½″ square.

2. Sew 2 aqua/red half-circle blocks to the right and left sides of an aqua 3½″ × 6½″ rectangle.

3. Sew an aqua 27½″ × 3½″ rectangle to the top and bottom of the unit from Step 2.

4. Sew the unit from Step 1 to the left side of the unit from Step 3.

5. Sew an aqua 3½″ × 12½″ rectangle to the right side of the unit from Step 4.

6. Sew a cream 6½″ × 6½″ square to the right side of a cream/red half-circle block.

7. Sew a cream 18½″ × 3½″ rectangle to the top and the bottom of the unit from Step 6.

8. Sew the unit from Step 7 to the right side of the unit from Step 4 to complete section A.

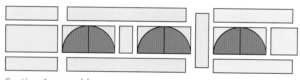

Section A assembly

Section B

Please refer to the Section B assembly diagram (next page).

1. Sew 3 chartreuse 3½″ × 3½″ squares and 3 white 3½″ × 3½″ squares together, alternating colors. Make 3.

2. Sew a chartreuse 3½″ × 9½″ rectangle to the white end of the unit from Step 1. Make 3.

3. Sew a pink 3½″ × 3½″ square to the bottom of each door block, including the plain charcoal 3½″ × 6½″ rectangles. For the two-color door blocks, place the color on the right side of the block. Make a total of 15 pink door units.

4. Sew an aqua 3½˝ × 3½˝ square to the top of a pink 3½˝ × 24½˝ rectangle. Make 3.

5. Sew a white 3½˝ × 3½˝ square to the top of a pink 3½˝ × 24½˝ rectangle. Make 3.

6. Following the diagram, sew the above units together with an aqua 3½˝ × 27½˝ rectangle, 3 chartreuse 3½˝ × 27½˝ rectangles, and a chartreuse 6½˝ × 27½˝ rectangle to complete section B.

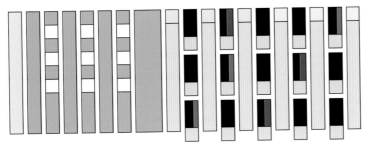

Section B assembly

Section C

Please refer to the Section C assembly diagram (below).

1. Sew an aqua 15½˝ × 3½˝ rectangle to the top of a cream 15½˝ × 3½˝ rectangle.

2. Sew the unit from Step 1 to the left side of a pink 18½˝ × 6½˝ rectangle.

3. Sew a cream 9½˝ × 3½˝ rectangle to the left side of a pink 27½˝ × 3½˝ rectangle. Make 2.

4. Sew the units from Step 3 together with 3 turquoise rectangles 27½˝ × 3½˝, alternating colors.

5. Sew a cream 6½˝ × 15½˝ rectangle to the left side of the unit from Step 4.

6. Following the diagram, sew the 2 units together to complete section C.

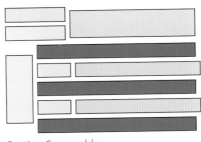

Section C assembly

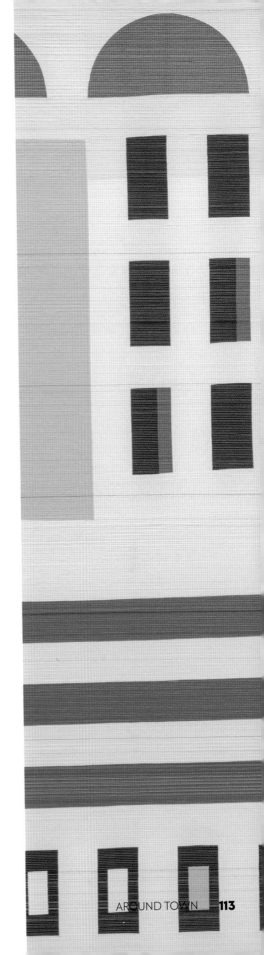

Section D

Please refer to the Section D assembly diagram (below).

1. Sew 2 cream 21½″ × 3½″ rectangles end to end. Make 2.

2. Following the diagram, sew together 7 cream 3½″ × 6½″ rectangles and 7 window blocks, alternating units.

3. Sew the cream units from Step 1 to the top and bottom of the unit from Step 2 to complete section D.

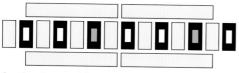

Section D assembly

Section E

Please refer to the Section E assembly diagram (below).

1. Sew a pink 3½″ × 6½″ rectangle to the left and right sides of a pink / red / white double half-circle block.

2. Sew a cream 3½″ × 6½″ rectangle to the left and right sides of a red half-circle block.

3. Sew a cream 3½″ × 6½″ rectangle to the left and right sides of a cream / red / turquoise double half-circle block.

4. Following the diagram, sew the units from Steps 1–3 together with 2 pink 18½″ × 6½″ rectangles and a cream 18½″ × 3½″ rectangle to complete section E.

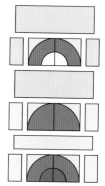

Section E assembly

QUILT ASSEMBLY

Following the quilt assembly diagram, sew sections A, B, C, D, and E to complete the quilt top.

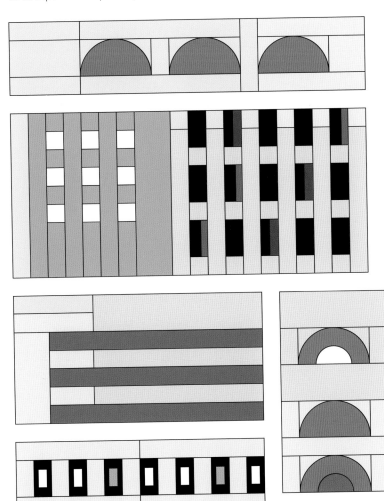

Quilt assembly

Detail of *Around Town*, showing the binding

Finishing

1. Divide the backing into 2 lengths. Sew the panels crosswise. The seam will be horizontal across the back of the quilt.

2. Layer, quilt, and bind as desired.

Around Town, 60″ × 72″, designed, pieced, and quilted by Heather Black

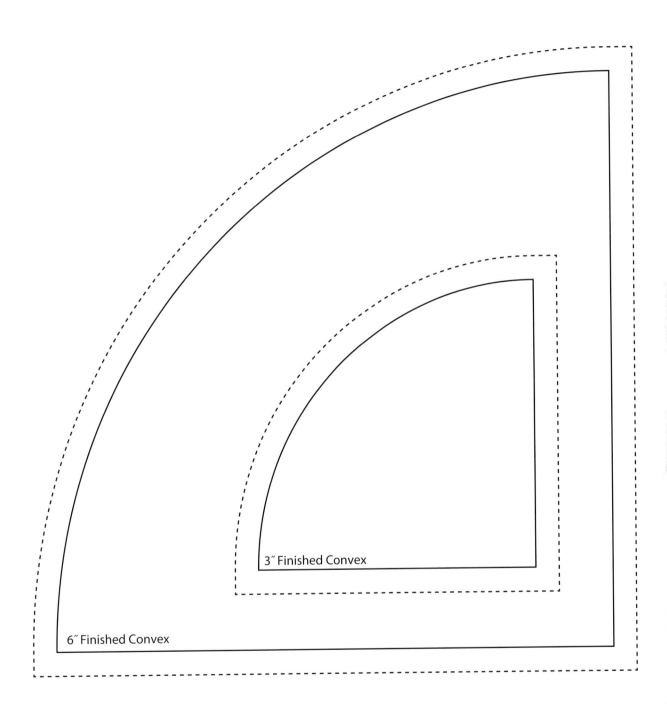

3″ Finished Convex

6″ Finished Convex

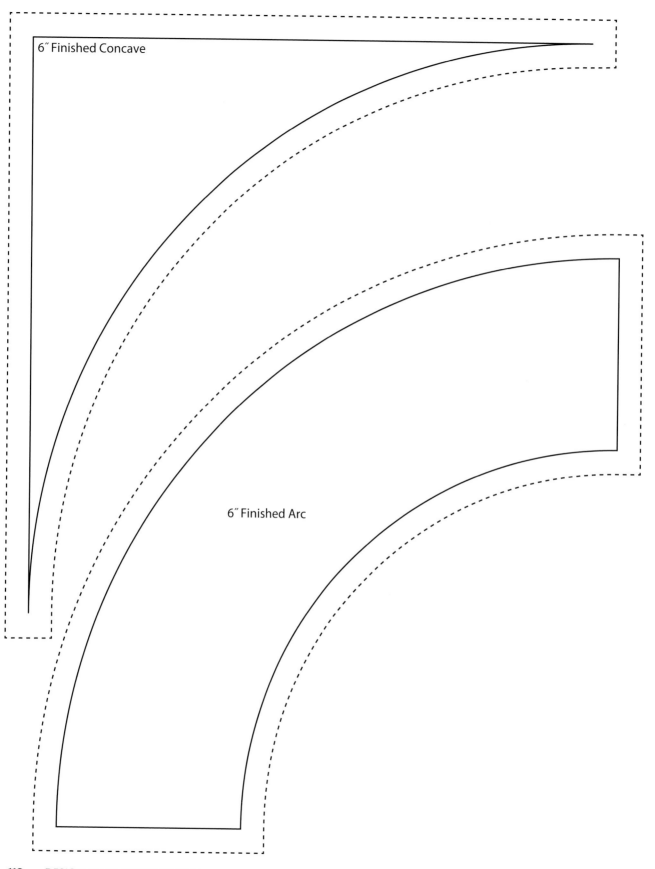

6″ Finished Concave

6″ Finished Arc

MISPRINT

FINISHED BLOCK: BASED ON A 4″ GRID

FINISHED QUILT: 60″ × 72″

MATERIALS

Yardages are based on 40″ usable width.

AQUA (Aruba*): 4½ yards, binding included

NAVY (Midnight*): 1¼ yards

RED 1 (Vintage Red*): ¼ yard

RED 2 (Christmas Red*): ¼ yard

RED 3 (Tomato*): ⅓ yard

ORANGE 1 (Carrot*): ⅓ yard

ORANGE 2 (Tangerine*): ⅓ yard

ORANGE 3 (Clementine*): ⅓ yard

YELLOW 1 (Daisy*): ⅓ yard

YELLOW 2 (Maize*): ¼ yard

BACKING (Navy**): 3⅞ yards for backing

BATTING: Twin size (I recommend Hobbs Tuscany Cotton/Wool Batting.)

> **Fabrics I used:**   * *Painter's Palette Solids by Paintbrush Studio Fabrics*
> ** *Wonder Joy by Paintbrush Studio Fabrics*

CUTTING

Make templates from these patterns: 4″ Concave (page 125) and 4″ Convex (page 125).
Cut the convex, concave, and arc units using the templates.

Aqua

• Cut 4 strips 16½″ × width of fabric. Subcut:

  2 rectangles 16½″ × 36½″ for right border

  2 rectangles 16½″ × 22½″ for bottom border

• Cut 12 strips 4½″ × width of fabric. Subcut:

  103 concave pieces

  31 squares 4½″ × 4½″

• Cut 8 strips 2½″ × width of fabric for binding.

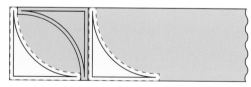

Concave cutting

Navy

• Cut 9 strips 4½″ × width of fabric. Subcut:

  20 concave pieces

  60 convex pieces

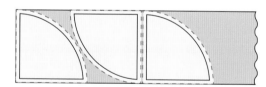

Convex cutting

Red 1

• Cut 1 convex piece.

Red 2

• Cut 1 strip 4½″ × width of fabric. Subcut
  4 convex pieces.

Red 3

• Cut 1 strip 4½″ × width of fabric. Subcut 8 convex pieces.

Orange 1

• Cut 2 strips 4½″ × width of fabric. Subcut 12 convex pieces.

Orange 2

• Cut 2 strips 4½″ × width of fabric. Subcut 14 convex pieces.

Orange 3

• Cut 2 strips 4½″ × width of fabric. Subcut 12 convex pieces.

Yellow 1

• Cut 1 strip 4½″ × width of fabric. Subcut 8 convex pieces.

Yellow 2

• Cut 1 strip 4½″ × width of fabric. Subcut 4 convex pieces.

CONSTRUCTION

Shadow Units

Sew a navy convex unit to an aqua concave unit, right sides together, by following these steps.

1. Mark the center of the convex unit by folding the unit in half along the curve and finger-pressing a crease. Do the same for the concave unit.

2. Place the concave unit on top of the convex unit right sides together.

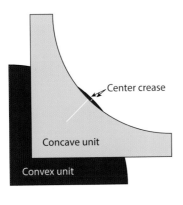

3. Line up the center creases and pin.

4. Finish by pinning along the curve as needed.

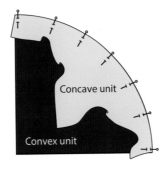

5. Sew along the curve with a scant ¼″ seam allowance, removing the pins as you sew.

6. Press the seam open creating 1 quarter-circle unit.

7. Repeat Steps 1–6 to make a total of 60 aqua/navy quarter-circle units.

Color Quarter-Circles

Repeat Steps 1–6 in the Shadow Units construction to make color quarter-circle units with the following convex and concave piece.

CONVEX	CONCAVE	NUMBER OF QUARTER-CIRCLE UNITS
Red 1	Navy	1
Red 2	Navy	2
Red 2	Aqua	2
Red 3	Navy	3
Red 3	Aqua	5
Orange 1	Navy	4
Orange 1	Aqua	8
Orange 2	Navy	4
Orange 2	Aqua	10
Orange 3	Navy	3
Orange 3	Aqua	9
Yellow 1	Navy	2
Yellow 1	Aqua	6
Yellow 2	Navy	1
Yellow 2	Aqua	3

Dot Blocks

Using the shadow quarter-circles, color quarter-circles, and aqua 4½˝ squares, assemble all the quarter-dot blocks, bottom half-dot blocks, right half-dot blocks, and full dot blocks.

Quarter-Dot Block

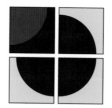

Make 1 using the red 1 unit.

Bottom Half-Dot Blocks

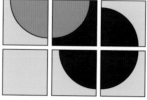

Make 3 total, 1 each using these color units: red 2, red 3, and orange 1.

Right Half-Dot Blocks

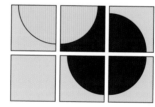

Make 4 total, 1 each using these color units: red 2, red 3, orange 1, and orange 2.

Full Dot Blocks

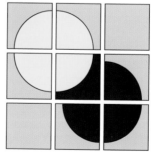

Make 12 total. Make 1 each using the red 3 and yellow 1 color units. Make 2 each using the orange 1 and yellow 1 color units. Make 3 each from the orange 2 and orange 3 color units.

Borders

1. Sew 2 bottom border strips 16½˝ × 22½˝ end to end to make 1 bottom border strip 16½˝ × 44½˝.

2. Sew 2 right border strips 16½˝ × 36½˝ end to end to make 1 right border strip 16½˝ × 72½˝.

Quilt Assembly

1. Following the diagram, sew the blocks into rows, then sew the rows together to complete the body of the quilt.

2. Sew the bottom border to the quilt.

3. Add the right border to complete the top.

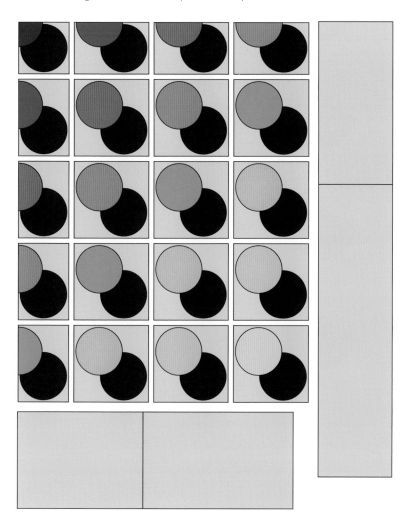

Finishing

1. Divide the backing into 2 lengths. Sew the panels crosswise. The seam will be horizontal across the back of the quilt.

2. Layer, quilt, and bind as desired.

Misprint, 60″ × 72″, designed, pieced, and quilted by Heather Black

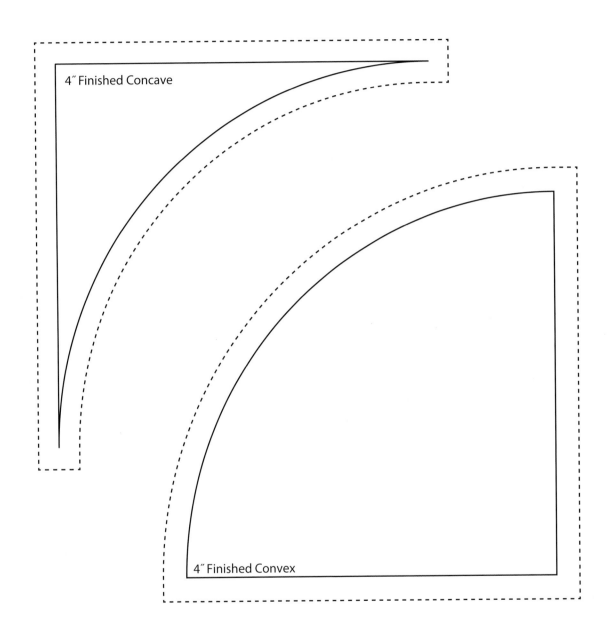

4″ Finished Concave

4″ Finished Convex

ABOUT THE AUTHOR

Heather Black first tried quilting in 1995 but didn't catch the quilting bug until 2011 when she designed, pieced, and hand quilted her first queen-sized quilt. Shortly after that, she discovered modern quilting and from that point on Heather has been designing and making quilts whenever possible.

Heather and her friend Daisy Aschehoug published their first book, *Quilt Modern Curves & Bold Stripes*, with C&T Publishing. She also has published an assortment of contemporary and modern quilt patterns, which have been featured in various quilting publications.

A myriad of Heather's quilts have been displayed at international, national, and regional quilt shows. Her quilts have hung at International Quilt Festival, Houston and Chicago; AQS Fall QuiltWeek; QuiltCon; MQX Midwest; and many more. Her quilt *Urban Trek* won first place for use of negative space at QuiltCon 2018 and she also has won several ribbons in regional and local shows.

Heather is a widowed mom of a beautiful girl, CoraJoan, and lives in Spokane, Washington. She grew up in the Pacific Northwest and attended college in Pennsylvania.

Visit Heather online and follow on social media!

Website: quiltachusetts.com

Instagram: @quiltachusetts

Also by Heather Black and Daisy Aschehoug:

Want even more creative content?

Visit us online at ctpub.com

FREE PATTERNS | FREE VIDEO TUTORIALS | TOOLS | GIFTS & MORE!

quilt, snap, share